A CHILD *is* BORN

A Child Is Born
A Beginner's Guide to Nativity Stories

A Child Is Born
978-1-7910-3510-5
978-1-7910-3511-2 *eBook*

A Child Is Born: DVD
978-1-7910-3514-3

A Child Is Born: Leader Guide
978-1-7910-3512-9
978-1-7910-3513-6 *eBook*

Also by Amy-Jill Levine

Short Stories by Jesus:
The Enigmatic Parables of a
Controversial Rabbi

Entering the Passion of Jesus:
A Beginner's Guide
to Holy Week

Light of the World:
A Beginner's Guide
to Advent

Sermon on the Mount:
A Beginner's Guide to the
Kingdom of Heaven

The Difficult Words of Jesus:
A Beginner's Guide to His
Most Perplexing Teachings

Witness at the Cross:
A Beginner's Guide
to Holy Friday

Signs and Wonders:
A Beginner's Guide to the
Miracles of Jesus

The Gospel of Mark:
A Beginner's Guide
to the Good News

The Gospel of John:
A Beginner's Guide to the Way,
the Truth, and the Light

With Warren Carter
The New Testament:
Methods and Meanings

With Marc Zvi Brettler
The Bible With
and Without Jesus:
How Jews and Christians
Read the Same Stories
Differently

AMY-JILL LEVINE

A CHILD
is BORN

A BEGINNER'S GUIDE TO NATIVITY STORIES

Abingdon Press | Nashville

A Child Is Born
A Beginner's Guide to Nativity Stories

Library of Congress Control Number: 2025939707
978-1-7910-3510-5

Cover description: *A Child is Born: A Beginner's Guide to Nativity Stories* by Amy-Jill Levine. The cover features a close-up image of a statue of Mary holding the baby Jesus, both with serene expressions. Mary wears a blue-green robe, and the baby is wrapped in a light cloth.

MANUFACTURED IN THE UNITED STATES OF AMERICA

For Maria Mayo
Mother, Daughter, Friend.

CONTENTS

View a complimentary session
of Amy-Jill Levine's
A Child Is Born.

Scan the QR code below or visit
https://tinyurl.com/yv392y8v

INTRODUCTION

Most Advent books start with Matthew 1–2 and Luke 1–2 and adduce earlier materials as background. For the First Gospel, they show how Matthew 1:23 uses the Greek translation of Isaiah 7:14, "Look, the virgin shall become pregnant and give birth to a son," to explain Mary's pregnancy before she and Joseph married. They show how Matthew constructs Jesus as a new Moses: endangered as a child, entering and leaving Egypt, crossing water, facing temptation in the wilderness, and ascending a mountain to teach. For Luke, they talk about how the conception of John, later titled "Baptizer," "Immerser," or for the less reverent, "Dunker," to the elderly and righteous Elizabeth and Zechariah resembles the miraculous conceptions of sons to elderly parents in the Scriptures of Israel, including Abraham and Sarah, the parents of Isaac; Manoah and Mrs. Manoah (Judges 13 gives her no name), the parents of the judge Samson; and Elkanah and Hannah, the parents of the prophet Samuel. They demonstrate how Hannah's prayer of exultation forms the model for Mary's Magnificat.

This volume instead foregrounds the earlier material to show its relevance to contemporary readers on its own terms. I've found in numerous church settings that congregants not only know the Gospel stories better than they know the stories in the Old Testament but also that they may not know those Old Testament stories at all. (By the way, I think the term "Old

Testament" for the Christian Bible Part I is a fine term, as long as we remember that "old" carries the connotations of "foundational," "bedrock," "grounding," and "of utmost value"). This lack of familiarity disturbs me, for these earlier stories were the grounding, the bedrock, for Jesus and his immediate followers.

A few times, I've heard such comments as, "I don't like the Old Testament with its angry and wrathful God." It appears that they've missed, among others, the stories of Hagar, Abraham, Ishmael and Isaac, Moses, his sister, his mother, Pharaoh's daughter, and two extraordinarily courageous midwives, and Manoah, Mrs. Manoah, an interesting and invested angel, and Samson, as well as Elkanah, Hannah, Samuel, and Eli the priest. They've probably also missed—in the New Testament—Jesus condemning people to the outer darkness, John demonizing his opponents as children of Satan, and most of the Book of Revelation (but here I am quibbling).

This study is not an exercise in compare and contrast, which would be more like a middle-school exam than a thoughtful reading of the Bible. It seeks rather to reveal what the comparison makes apparent, including surprise over the echoes of one text by another, wonder at the emotions the stories evoke, and delight in the nuances of the ancient Hebrew of the Old Testament (or as Jews refer to this collection, the Tanakh) and its Greek translation.

The Bible has numerous chapters that could be titled "A Child Is Born." Eve gives birth to Cain, Abel, and Seth. Both Cain and Seth marry (explanations for where they found wives will have to wait for another volume) and become fathers and grandfathers. Noah and Mrs. Noah (the Bible often omits the names of wives and mothers) have three sons, who have wives, who have children. There are many more examples in the Old Testament, and the New Testament adds to them. Matthew begins with a genealogy, which in the seventeenth-century King James Version is a series of begats: "Abraham begat Isaac; and Isaac begat Jacob; and Jacob begat Judas and his brethren" (Matthew 1:2). (Those who claim this is the "Authorized Version" are correct, although it helps to note that it was the King of England who authorized it.) In each generation, children are born.

Stories of the conception and birth of Jesus, found in the Gospels of Matthew and Luke, draw upon earlier accounts of angelic annunciations, divine involvement in human activities, frightened parents and endangered children. Each story can stand on its own. Yet, when read with the knowledge of the Old Testament stories, each becomes more meaningful.

Connections of New Testament material to Old Testament stories and, as we'll see, even the myths of ancient Greek and Mediterranean cultures should be cause for celebration, not worry. Good stories are good stories, no matter who tells them. One of the reasons the Christian message was able to take root in both Jewish and pagan contexts was because it consisted of stories that would have been familiar to each group. For just one quick example, Revelation 12:1-6 states, "A great portent appeared in heaven: a woman clothed with the sun, with the moon under her feet, and on her head a crown of twelve stars. She was pregnant and was crying out in birth pangs, in the agony of giving birth." When a great red dragon attempts to devour the newborn, who is destined to rule all nations, "her child was snatched away and taken to God and to his throne." The woman then flees to the wilderness, where she is protected. The story alludes to Jesus and Mary, but it also bears traces of the birth of Zeus's children Apollo and Artemis to Leto, and Leto's persecution by Hera, Zeus's jealous wife.

In interpreting such material, we can take a cue from Paul. According to Acts 17, in his speech in Athens (at the Areopagus, or "Mars Hill"), Paul cites from Posidonius of Rhodes, who lived in a century before Jesus, and from Aratus, a poet who lived two centuries before him.

Indeed, knowing the earlier stories would have made the books in the New Testament more interesting to their first audiences, and they should have the same impact on present-day readers. The Christmas stories are familiar, perhaps too familiar. For example, most of us recall the angel Gabriel's visit with Mary, who wonders about how she is going to conceive a child given her lack of experience (a G-rated description), but fewer know that both her doubts and her amazement have precedent in the stories of the conception of Isaac to Sarah and Abraham, and of Samson to Mrs. Manoah and her husband. We recall the camaraderie between Elizabeth and Mary, two pregnant Jewish women. Their relationship evokes a variation on the themes of rival mothers, including Hagar and Sarah, Leah and Rachel, Penninah and Hannah. Concerns regarding Abraham's fathering a child echo in the stories of Manoah, the father of Samson, and then Joseph, the (legal) father of Jesus.

Type Scenes

Such stories fit distinct literary conventions or *type scenes*, just as today we can classify shows by genre: the procedural (*CSI, NCIS, Law and Order*), apocalyptic dystopia (*The Living Dead, The Last of Us*), situation comedies (from *The Honeymooners* to *The Flintstones* to *The Jetsons* and numerous variants). We enjoy the variations on the theme. For the Gospels to replay Old Testament scenes is not plagiarizing; to the contrary, repetition of conventions both shows respect for the earlier stories and anchors Jesus into the history of his people.

The birth stories—or nativity narratives—follow two major conventions. The first is the pregnancy of a woman who has suffered fertility problems. Genesis 18:9-15 tells of how Sarah, at age ninety (bless her heart!), gives birth to her one and only child, Isaac. Chapter 1 of this book reveals the multiple messages this story contains. In Genesis 25:19-26, Isaac prays on behalf of his wife, Rebekah, that God will open her womb (the biblical default is that wombs are "closed" until God acts to open them) and grant her a child. Rebekah gives birth to fraternal twins, Esau and Jacob. In the next generation, Jacob's less-loved wife Leah easily conceives and gives birth; the beloved but infertile Rachel demands that Jacob "Give me children or I shall die" (Genesis 30:1). God then opens her womb, and Rachel bears Joseph (he of *Amazing Technicolor Dreamcoat* fame). Rachel will then die giving birth to Joseph's brother Benjamin (this story of maternal mortality reappears in the narrative of the prophet Samuel's childhood, when the priest Eli's daughter-in-law dies giving birth).

Another example, and the focus of chapter 2 of this book, is the story in Judges 13 of Manoah and his wife, whose infertility the story mentions frequently. Mrs. Manoah becomes the mother of the judge Samson. The focus of chapter 3 is the story of Hannah, another co-wife, who according to 1 Samuel 1 becomes the mother of the prophet Samuel. Finally, the "wealthy woman" serves as the patron to the prophet Elisha. The Hebrew actually describes her as *gedolah vatachzeq*, "big and strong." I picture her less as dripping in jewels than as able to bench-press the prophet. This unnamed "Great Woman" of Shunem conceives an unnamed son (2 Kings 4:8-17). These scenes find their New Testament counterpart in the elderly Elizabeth and Zechariah.

The second nativity convention is the annunciation: a message, often but not always delivered by an angel, that a woman, often one suffering from infertility, will conceive a child whose fate is then predicted. Lists of Old Testament annunciations usually begin with Genesis 18, the notice given by three visitors to Abraham that his wife Sarah (at this point called Abram and Sarai, but we'll identify them by their better-known names) will have a son. I prefer to include an earlier annunciation, this one to Hagar, the enslaved woman who, because of Sarah's machinations, is pregnant with Abraham's child. In Genesis 16, Hagar flees from Sarah's abuse. She is alone, pregnant, and without food or water. But in this desperate setting, she encounters an angel who makes predictions concerning her son. Hagar's story is also featured in chapter 1.

The third annunciation, like that of the angel to Hagar, also occurs not before but during the pregnancy. Rebekah fears that the pregnancy is going to kill her. God then explains, "Two nations are in your womb" (Genesis 25:23), but the older will serve the younger. This is not great prenatal news, and it impacts how both Rebekah and Isaac parent their children. Nor do we ever learn if Rebekah shared this news with her husband.

The annunciation motif returns a fourth time in Judges 13 with the conception and birth of Samson, as we see in chapter 2 of this book. A hint of the motif, the fifth here and the focus of chapter 3, surfaces in 1 Samuel 1:17, when the priest Eli sees the fervent prayer of the (again, infertile) Hannah (he thinks she is drunk, because her lips are moving in prayer but she is making no sounds). When she corrects him, he makes the annunciation, "The God of Israel grant the petition you have made to him." She will then give birth to the prophet Samuel.

Sixth, we return in 2 Kings 4 with the "big and strong" Shunamite woman. When Elisha asks his servant Gehazi what he might to do reciprocate her hospitality, the servant not-too-subtly hints, "Well, she has no son, and her husband is old" (2 Kings 4:14). Whether Gehazi suggests that Elisha arrange a miracle (it would not be the first time) or that Elisha should be proactive given the husband's enervated state is up to readers to decide. Elisha asks Gezahi to call the woman, and when she arrives, the prophet announces that she will, next year, embrace a son. The woman responds with the same incredulity that marked Sarah's reaction to the annunciation that she, at age ninety, will bear a son. But the Shunamite woman, unlike Sarah, does not laugh; instead, she accuses Elisha of lying to her cruelly. The next verse, 2 Kings 4:17, proves the prophet did not lie.

A seventh annunciation, although not always included in the list, is Isaiah's famous notice of a sign to King Ahaz: he is to observe a pregnant young woman (Hebrew *almah*) and know that before her son, who will be named Immanuel (Hebrew for "God is with us"), comes to moral awareness, the king's political problems will evaporate. When Isaiah 7:14 is translated into Greek (the Septuagint), the Hebrew term *almah*, "young woman" is read as *parthenos*, "virgin," and this translation underlies the virginal conception in Matthew's Nativity account.

No annunciation marks the birth of either Moses or David, and the lack of this convention may indicate the fraught relationship they have with the deity, including feelings of being overwhelmed and even abandoned. While David lacks a birth story, the conception and birth of Moses is told in some detail in Exodus 1–2, and these stories, too, find their connections in Matthew's Nativity account. On the other hand, both Moses and David fit the biblical convention of preferring younger children over older siblings (as an only child, I have no horse in this race). Moses is the younger brother of Miriam and Aaron; David is Jesse's seventh son. This motif is hinted at in Luke's Nativity story, where John the Baptizer plays the role of the older brother, and again "the older will serve the younger." The absence of annunciations for Moses and David also informs us that conception does not require angelic hooplah; we are all children of God.

That Luke and Matthew draw from the Scriptures of Israel is very old news. Less familiar is how the variations on the themes bring out additional meanings that can help us in thinking about Advent. These fascinating stories, with their common themes and their major differences, seem to me like part of an orchestral score. The strings and the wind instruments can play a beautiful tune on their own, but when put together, a harmonious and much more gorgeous production occurs.

Outline of *A Child Is Born*

Chapter 1 looks at the conceptions of Abraham's two children. The first son is Ishmael, born to Hagar, who is both enslaved to Sarah, Abraham's wife, and is also a wife of Abraham (one needs a scorecard to keep track of who's who in this family). The second son is Isaac, Sarah's only child. These stories from Genesis 16 (Ishmael) and 21 (Isaac) open multiple questions: of the importance of motherhood in ancient Israel and so today; of how to address infertility, another issue that crosses the centuries. The stories also speak of what happens when a parent loves one child more than another and when jealousies arise in blended families. The story of Hagar and Sarah, rival co-wives, repeats in the stories of Rachel and Leah, and then again in the story of Hannah and Peninnah (to which we return in chapter 3). Elizabeth and Mary, the older and younger cousins, evoke even as they break the pattern. Hagar and Sarah, Ishmael and Isaac, also move us to Paul, who in Galatians 4 reads their story as an an allegory. Finally, we can read the cousins John and Jesus as potential rivals, but in their case, rivalries are again overcome.

Chapter 2 brings us to Samson. (I have warm thoughts of Victor Mature and Hedy Lamarr in the 1949 Cecil B. DeMille blockbuster *Samson and Delilah*. Ironically, Victor Mature, who played Samson, was a cradle Roman Catholic, while Hedy Lamarr, who played Delilah, had Jewish parents. But I digress.) The meeting between Mrs. Manoah (the Book of Judges names Samson's father, not his mother) and an angel, and the subsequent encounter of Manoah with the same angel, shows that annunciations can be funny.

There are good reasons for thinking that the angel has something to do with Samson's conception, including the tradition of "fallen" angels marrying human women (see Genesis 6:1-4) and the extraordinary (superhuman) strength that Samson will later display. Not everyone can kill three thousand soldiers with a donkey's jawbone or can pull down a temple (Samson "brought down the house") single-handedly. The story helps us see just how amazing, even bizarre, the involvement of the divine in human conception can be, and so the story helps us re-see both the joy and the mystery in the New Testament Nativity accounts.

Chapter 3 concerns the annunciation to Hannah, the mother of Samuel. Whereas most Advent stories concentrate on her prayer in 1 Samuel 2, the prototype for Mary's Magnificat (Luke 1:46-56), we focuses on Hannah's role prior to the conception and birth of her child. We also attend to Hannah's sympathetic husband Elkanah, a prototype of Joseph, the husband of Mary. Hannah will dedicate her son Samuel to God at the shrine at Shiloh, as Mary presents Jesus to God in the Jerusalem Temple according to Luke 2. Eli the priest becomes Samuel's foster father, and Elkanah steps aside. Joseph will replay this scene, when Jesus informs him that he must be in his "Father's house" (Luke 2:49) or, more literally, "about matters concerning my Father": Jesus's "Father" here is God, not Joseph.

For me, the Old Testament texts have personal meaning. Regarding the first two: In the synagogue, on the first day of Rosh Ha-Shanah, the Jewish new year, the Torah (the Pentateuch, the five books of Moses) reading is Genesis 21:1-34, the story of Isaac's birth and then the expulsion of Ishmael and Hagar from their home with Abraham and Sarah. The reading from the Prophets (known as the *haftarah*) is 1 Samuel 1:1–2:10, the story of Hannah and Samuel. There are multiple reasons. Both concern infertility that is resolved with new life and new possibilities. Both model prayer, with Hagar praying for the life of her son Ishmael, and with Hannah, in her first recorded words, addressing God as "Lord of Hosts" and asking that he remember her. I like to think that the stories from Genesis and 1 Samuel were assigned for this day because both focus on families: not just men, but also women and children. They thus speak to the tradition's communal dimensions.

Judges 13 was my daughter Sarah's *haftarah* passage when she, many years ago, became bat mitzvah. The Torah reading paired with this passage in Numbers 12, the "test of bitter waters" that was, during the wilderness period, to be administered to a woman suspected of adultery. In her *d'var Torah* (lit. "word of Torah," here indicating a homily or reflection) on Numbers 12 and Judges 13 for the congregation, Sarah suggested that the ancient rabbis put these texts together to suggest that any man who would humiliate his wife by publicly accusing her of adultery is to be seen as slow-witted as Manoah, Samson's (reputed) father. Could be.

Finally, one more personal note. My parents were married eighteen years before I was born, and my mother suffered several miscarriages. When she was forty-three, she went to her doctor because she felt that something was off. After running the usual tests, her doctor informed her that she was pregnant. My mother (channeling the "great woman" of Shunem), was livid: "How dare you joke with me about something like that!" She booked an appointment with another physician. The first doctor called my father to tell him the good news, and only when she heard that news from my father did my mother believe the story. She was forty-four when I was born, and I am an only child. I take these stories personally. Children born in such circumstances may be particularly well parented (I was); they may feel a particular concern to honor their parents by their actions (I do).

Chapter 4 returns us to Jesus as well as to Mary and Joseph, who have been present throughout our discussion. Here we discover how reading Matthew 1–2 and Luke 1–2 in light of the earlier conceptions and births gives new meaning to the Christmas story. More, in light of the Gospel stories, we gain new insights into these earlier texts.

Moses as Frame

For the rest of this introduction as well as the epilogue, we'll use the birth story of Moses to frame these other chapters. For Moses, there is neither an annunciation nor an infertile woman. To the contrary, at the beginning of the Exodus story, the Hebrew women are so fertile that Pharaoh, Egypt's king, fears that these immigrants will become so numerous that they will ally themselves with foreign nations and threaten Egypt's autonomy. Already this story finds connections to the stories we've already mentioned.

For example, Hagar's name suggests "not native born," "stranger," "alien," or "migrant." The Hebrew *ha* is the definite article "the"; *gēr* is the "not-native born." The term appears in Leviticus 19:34, "The alien [*hagēr*] who resides [*hagar*] with you shall be to you as the native-born among you; you shall love the alien (*hagēr*) as yourself, for you were aliens [*gērim*] in the land of Egypt." According to Leviticus 19:18, we are to love our neighbors as ourselves, because they are like us, fellow members of the same group. More, they are invested in the same social good as we are, hence they are neighbors. Leviticus 19:34 insists that we are to love the non-native born who dwells in our land, because we "were aliens in the land of Egypt." The first love command is based in identity; the second is based in experience.

Exodus 23:9 makes the point even stronger. The NRSVue reads, "You shall not oppress a resident alien; you know the heart of an alien, for you were aliens in the land of Egypt." The word translated "heart" is, in Hebrew, *nephesh*, which connotes "soul," or what animates a person (the Greek for *nephesh* is *psychē*, as in "psychology" or "psychiatry").

For another connection to Moses: in Genesis 16, Sarah abuses her Egyptian slave Hagar. The story finds a new iteration in Exodus, where the Egyptians enslave and then abuse Sarah's descendants, the children of Israel. Genesis 15:13 predicts this fate: God tells Abraham, "Your offspring shall be aliens [*gērim*] in a land that is not theirs and shall be slaves there, and they shall be oppressed for four hundred years." The term for "oppressed" (Hebrew *oni*; Greek *tapeinoō*), first used in the Bible here, returns in Genesis 16:9, when the angel tells Hagar, "Return to your mistress, and submit [that is, accept your role as one oppressed and humiliated (Hebrew *oni*; Greek *tapeinoō*)] to her."

Like Samson, Moses is a military leader, although he is known for neither long locks nor physical prowess. Like Samuel, he is a political leader whose people frequently reject him. Like Jesus, the connections among all these figure are manifold.

Each time we compare one text to another, we see things we had not seen before. More, the comparisons raise questions about responsibility and courage, prayers and vows, parents and children, fathers and mothers, being part of a community and being an individual. And each new light shines differently when it is turned to the Gospel stories of Jesus.

The Exodus Generation

At the end of the Book of Genesis, Joseph, who has become second-in-command in Egypt, relocates his entire family to an area in Egypt called the "Land of Goshen" (e.g., Genesis 45:10; I initially heard "land of Goshen" as "'Lantic Ocean" and concluded that this is why Egypt had water; apparently I was in denial [find the pun]). After detailing the children of Jacob (Israel) and their descendants, the Book of Exodus ominously notes that a new king arose over Egypt who did not know Joseph and so did not know how Joseph, an immigrant, saved Egypt's population from starvation during seven years of famine. In politics, today even more so than then, memories can be short. The irony is notable: The king who did not know Joseph's name is not named.

This new Pharaoh (the name means "Great House"; it is a metonymy, as in "the White House says") fears that the Israelites are becoming numerous and therefore politically dangerous. Despite their having been in Egypt for centuries and having shown nothing but loyalty to their new home, he fears they will ally themselves with Egypt's enemies. As a prophylactic measure, Pharaoh enslaves the Israelites and forces them to construct the two store-cities of Pithom and Rameses. However, "The more they were oppressed, the more they multiplied" (Exodus 1:12). This resilience creates fear in the hearts of the Egyptians. Rather than seek rapprochement, the Egyptians increase the hardships of slavery.

Then the horror becomes more horrific. Pharaoh summons the "Hebrew midwives Shiprah and Puah" and commands them to kill every boy that emerges from an Israelite womb (Exodus 1:16). That the population relied on only two midwives does not suggest, at least to me, that they were all that numerous, but given the king's agenda, facts are irrelevant.

The midwives, in a striking act of disobedience, refuse: "But the midwives feared God; they did not do as the king of Egypt commanded them, but they let the boys live" (Exodus 1:17).

The text prompts questions of medical attention, cowardice and courage, and of wisdom and stupidity. For example, the

Introduction

New Testament Nativity stories say nothing about midwives.
The second-century Christian text known as the *Protevangelium*
(i.e., "pre-Gospel") *of James*, which describes Mary's conception
and birth, childhood, marriage to Joseph, and then the birth
of Jesus, mentions a midwife in relation to Mary's pregnancy.
Doubting that a virgin could not only conceive but also give
birth, the midwife performs a gynecological test on Mary. The
midwife's hand then shrivels, and it is healed only when she
touches baby Jesus. Aside from this fanciful story, the midwives
in Exodus prompt me to ask, who was with Elizabeth and who
was with Mary when they each gave birth to their sons? Even
today, we may well ignore the people who provide medical aid
and emotional comfort. For those who have had children: do
we remember the names of the doctor and nursing staff? Did we
consider using a midwife or a doula?

Cowardice not only marks Pharaoh, fearful that immigrants will destroy his culture (as if it were not strong enough
to prevail), it marks the Egyptian population as well. Tyrants
do not work on their own. The king first gets his native population to agree to the enslavement: "Look," he tells them, "the
Israelite people are more numerous and more powerful than
we" (Exodus 1:9). They were not as powerful, for if they were,
they would have required more than two midwives, and they
would not have allowed themselves to be enslaved. The king is,
it seems to me, interested in free labor, and he finds it expedient
to have "foreigners" do the work. He gains the Egyptians' support by giving them a common enemy. Not only the king, but
all the Egyptians ruthlessly increased the workload imposed on
the Israelites (Exodus 1:13-14).

The midwives represent the courage that the general population should have manifested. More, they beat the king at his own game of dehumanization by dissembling, "The Hebrew women are not like the Egyptian women, for they are vigorous and give birth before the midwife comes to them" (Exodus 1:19). The king wants to think of the Israelites as somehow subhuman, and the midwives play into his claims: yes, indeed, they are like animals, not like (delicate) Egyptian women.

As far as political policy, the king's order that the boys be killed is ridiculous. The odds of population growth are much better with ten women and one man (ideally I do not need to explain the math) than with ten men and one woman. Thus, the story tells us to attend to women, Israelite mothers and daughters, and the midwives. This focus on women will continue in the next scene, the conception, birth, and early childhood of Moses. It will continue in the Gospel of Luke, with its focus on Elizabeth and then on Mary.

The end of this opening vignette in Exodus is the notice that "God dealt well with the midwives....And because the midwives feared God, he gave them families" (1:20-21). The beginning of Exodus omits the name of the king, of Moses's mother and father and sister, and of Pharaoh's daughter who rescues Moses from death. Only the names of the midwives are recorded.

Again, I am reminded of the Gospel accounts. We have the names of Herod and Gabriel, Mary and Joseph (plus two full and differing genealogies for him, genealogies reminiscent of the opening of Exodus). But we do not know the names of the magi in Matthew's Gospel: Melchior, Gaspar (or Caspar), and Balthazar are from early Church tradition. Nor do we have the names of the shepherds in Luke. Whose names are recorded, and for what reason? When do we lump groups together (Israelites, Egyptians, Pharisees, scribes), and when do we focus on individuals? Do individuals disrupt stereotypes? Or, are they exceptions that prove the rule?

The midwives show that individuals can do something to stop oppression. At the same time, the mention of their names highlights all those unnamed people who colluded with the Israelites' enslavement, whether out of fear or lack of concern or delight in the free labor. We tend to remember the heroes, the ones who stood apart. Sometimes by thinking about them, we can more easily ignore the culpable majority. Here I think of those soldiers who, upon the orders of King Herod the Great, slaughtered the babies in Bethlehem to kill the baby Jesus (see Matthew 2). Did any rebel? Did they say that they were "just following orders"? The text both inspires and, often, indicts.

The Bible is honest about hardships and horrors: famine, displacement, enslavement, genocide. We could succumb to despair. Yet the authors of the biblical texts refused to see themselves only as victims; they recognized their agency, and they retained the view that the God of Abraham, Isaac, Jacob, Sarah, Rebekah, Rachel, and Leah, heard their cries.

As acts of resistance, they told stories not just of the Egyptians who promoted genocide; they told stories of Egyptians who defied the orders to kill. They told stories of resisting families, of mothers and daughters, who subverted the cruel practices of the state. And in these stories, they found a freedom that would inspire them through the millennia.

The Command to Genocide

Because Pharaoh's command that the midwives kill the babies did not resolve his concern, he enlists the Egyptian population not simply in enslaving the Israelites, but also in killing them. He "commanded *all* his people…"—not just the army, not just the workers, not just the men, but all, that "every son that is born you shall throw into the Nile, but you shall let every daughter live" (Exodus 1:22, my translation).

This verse presents what biblical scholars call a "text-critical" problem: Such problems occur when different manuscripts or translations have different readings. My translation above follows the Masoretic text, the Hebrew version standardized by Jewish communities in the ninth through eleventh centuries and the basis of all Torah scrolls produced today. Other ancient versions, including the Samaritan Pentateuch, the Septuagint (the Greek translation of a Hebrew original), and the Targums (the postbiblical Aramaic paraphrases of the Hebrew) clarify the command. Instead of reading, "Every son that is born you shall throw into the Nile," they offer, "Every son that is born *to the Hebrews* you shall throw into the Nile." Text-critics need to determine if this qualification dropped out of the Hebrew text or whether translators added it to make more sense of Pharaoh's command. As with many such discussions, scholars disagree.

My sense is that the Hebrew version, minus the qualification, is the original. It can be understood as having Pharaoh, depicted as rash and unthinking, ironically signing the death warrant for his own people. The other versions give the logical reading; the Hebrew gives the ironic, and also more truthful reading, for any country that issues warrants for genocide dooms itself. That doom comes in the tenth plague God inflicts on the Egyptians who enslaved Israel: death "from the firstborn of Pharaoh who sits on his throne to the firstborn of the female slave who is behind the handmill and all the firstborn of the livestock" (Exodus 11:5). This verse shows us that mistreatment is not limited to the wealthy and the healthy and that people who are themselves mistreated, such as Egypt's non-Israelite slaves, can also be guilty.

Much of the Torah is built on empathy, something in short supply in Egypt, and hardly only there. The point returns us to Leviticus 19:34, the command to love the *gēr*, the alien, or the immigrant.

Among the factors that prevent this love, as well as love of neighbor (Leviticus 19:18), which also requires self-love, are guilt, based in action (regret for what one has done), and shame, based in lack of self-worth (regret for who one is). The Exodus narrative helps us toward introspection. While today we may not be guilty of enslaving or murdering, we all bear some guilt through sins of commission (what we did) or, more likely, omission (what we failed to do, as in what "all the people" of Egypt, save the two midwives, failed to do).

We also may feel shame: that we are not good enough, talented enough, spiritual enough. I wonder if the Israelite husbands felt shame: They were unable to protect their wives and their sons. The topic moves me to Joseph. I wonder what Joseph thought when "an angel of the Lord appeared" to him "in a dream and said, 'Get up, take the child and his mother, and flee to Egypt, and remain there until I tell you, for Herod is about to search for the child, to destroy him.'" Joseph "took the child and his mother by night, and went to Egypt" (Matthew 2:13-14). He could have warned the other parents in Bethlehem. Did he feel guilt when he learned that Herod's soldiers slaughtered the children of his neighbors? Did he feel shame for not having done anything?

The good news here is twofold. First, the text forces us to confront ourselves, the ugly as well as the beautiful. It asks that we learn from our experiences and avoid rather than repeat the bad ones. Second, it shows us that patterns can be broken, and patterns become easier to break once we realize that they exist. We can learn to welcome people who are not of our "group," however defined, and it may turn out that their presence, rather than the threat that Pharaoh imagines, becomes a blessing.

Moses's Parents and Sister

I marvel at the Israelites' persistence and resilience. Immediately following Pharaoh's order, we learn that despite the enslavement and the order to kill babies, "A man from the house of Levi went and married a Levite woman" (Exodus 2:1). Nothing about their names, or how they were faring; all we have is their tribal identification. They vaguely remind us of Zechariah and Elizabeth, both from priestly families and so from the tribe of Levi.

Introduction

Following the notice of the marriage between these two Levites—we learn later that their names are Amram and Jochebed—Exodus 2:2a laconically notes, "The woman conceived and bore a son." Despite commands that children be killed, Amran and Jochebed continued to reproduce. Nothing here about their other children, Aaron and Miriam, who earlier had to have been conceived, carried to term, and born. This marriage between the two Levites and the subsequent birth of their son happens at a time when baby boys are being killed and the girls, like their parents, enslaved. The text implicitly raises the question of why anyone would, under such circumstances, risk having a child. And the rabbis take up the challenge by offering a midrash, an interpretation and elaboration of the biblical text. In the rabbinic reading (*b. Sotah* 12a), the Levite man, Amram, convinces his fellow Israelite men to divorce their wives. With no marriage, there will be no intercourse (so he supposes), and with no intercourse there will be no dead children. The divorce argument also explains how the narrative moves from the marriage of the Levite man and woman to the birth of Moses without mentioning Aaron and Miriam: Moses is the result of the remarriage after the divorce (the rabbis can be very clever!).

Miriam, who according to the midrash is at this time six years old, informs her father that his plan is worse that that of Pharaoh. While Pharaoh doomed the male babies, a decree preventing marriage and so preventing children dooms the entire next generation. Amram recognizes his daughter's wisdom; the men remarry their wives.

In some cases, where political leaders fail, children—indeed, daughters—may have the better ideas. According to another midrash also preserved in the *Babylonian Talmud* (*b. Bava Batra* 120a), Jochebed was 130 when she conceived Moses (surpassing the miracle for Sarah). When she remarried Amran, her wrinkles disappeared and she regained her youth.

Another text, this one in Latin, formally called *Liber Antiquitatum Biblicarum* but colloquially known as *Pseudo-Philo*, tells the same story, but here the elders advise divorce and Amram argues against it. If Pseudo-Philo wrote prior to the midrash, which is likely, then the rabbis enhanced the role of the daughter, Miriam.

Exodus 2:2, following the announcement of the birth, notes that when the (still unnamed) mother "saw that he was a fine [the Hebrew is *tov*, literally, 'good'] baby, she hid him three months." While various midrashim (the plural of midrash, as in "cherubim" and "seraphim") unpack what "good" indicates, from being born circumcised to having the room filled with light, I prefer to think of the mother here as epitomizing all parents who love their children: they are necessarily "good" because they are loved.

This mother is emotionally torn: on the one hand, she wants to keep the child with her; on the other, she recognizes that to preserve his life, she needs to let him be raised by others. She chooses, with courage, what is best for the child.

To preserve her baby's life, the mother constructs, with papyrus, bitumen, and pitch, what the NRSVue calls a "basket" but what the Hebrew identifies as a *tēvah*, an ark, the same term that describes the ship Noah constructed to preserve the animals and his family from the Flood. The universal disaster described in Genesis 6–9 is repeated, in Exodus 2, on the personal level. Nevertheless, as Noah's flood has universal import, so will this three-month-old baby in his tiny ark.

Moses's mother then takes the *tēvah* and places it among the reeds on the bank of the Nile. Technically, she has followed Pharaoh's commands. She has cast the child into the river; she simply did so by using an ark. The midwives deceive Pharaoh by stating that the Israelite women were too vigorous, too animalistic, to need their assistance; Moses's mother is similarly subverting the law through a ruse.

Ancient readers here would have recognized the conventions in this story. For example, one seventh century BCE Neo-Assyrian text (for comparison, this is the time following the destruction of the Northern Kingdom of Israel but before Babylon conquered the Southern Kingdom of Judah) describes Sargon, King of Akkad from the third millennium BCE, as the son of a high priestess and of an unknown father. His mother, after giving birth in secret, puts the baby into a basket of rushes with a bitumen seal and places the basket in the Euphrates River. A water-drawer named Akki finds the basket, rescues the baby, and raises him as his own son. Another version of this storyline has the Egyptian mother-goddess Isis place her son Horus in a papyrus thicket to hide him from the god Seth, who had killed her husband Osiris.

As Sargon is rescued by a water-drawer, so the Israelite baby is drawn from the water when Pharaoh's daughter, who had come to the river (the Nile, but like everyone else in Exodus 2 so far, unnamed) to bathe, orders her enslaved woman (Hebrew *amah*, the same word describing Hagar in Genesis 21:10,12-13) to bring the baby to her. One midrash in the *Babylonian Talmud, Sotah* 12b, states that when Pharaoh's daughter sought to rescue the baby, the women accompanying her warned her not to disobey her father's wishes. At this point, the angel Gabriel (the same angel who announces to Mary that she will bear a child) silences the women (the same angel who silences Zechariah when he doubts that he and Elizabeth would have a son) and encourages Pharaoh's daughter.

Filling out the story of Moses's conception and birth, Exodus tells us that the baby's sister, who had been watching the rescue, approaches the princess and asks her if she'd like to have a Hebrew woman nurse the child. The princess agrees, and so the baby's sister calls her own mother, the baby's mother, to nurse the baby.

Years pass, and when the child has grown, the mother returns the child to Pharaoh's daughter. Only here, at the end of the story, Exodus mentions that Pharaoh's daughter named the child Moses, the only name to be revealed in Exodus 2:1-10. The Hebrew text gives a false etymology in having the princess explain, "'because,' she said, 'I drew him out of the water'" (Exodus 2:10). Hebrew for "draw out" is *mashah*, which sounds like "Moses." The name is actually an Egyptian term for "gave birth to" and so "son of"; it appears in names like Rameses (son of [the god] Ra) and Thutmose (son of [the god] Toth). Egyptian origins may underlie the name of Moses's sister, which we shortly learn is "Miriam" (Mary is a cognate). In Egyptian, *meri* means "beloved"; it is usually followed by the name of a local god.

To ancient ears, the name Moses could have sounded both Egyptian and Hebrew, and his story will have implications for his fellow Israelites as well as for the Egyptians. His story tells us that political rebellion is not just among the midwives but in Pharaoh's own household. Not only his daughter, but also her enslaved women, disobey the order to drown the Israelite babies.

We can wonder what Moses's biological mother called him. We can wonder what she taught him about his own people, or what she hid from him in order to protect him. As with many biblical stories, the narrator often passes from the birth of the child to that child's adult status. We are free to fill in the details.

The story of the conception and birth of Moses leads us to Jesus, another endangered baby. Each story asks about the unsung heroes and the unnamed perpetrators. The Exodus story tells us that the Egyptians can be both benevolent and deadly, just as the Gospel stories give us the venal Jewish king Herod and the compassionate Jewish father Joseph. If we think of Egypt as a place of slavery, we know that, in the Joseph story, it was also a place of refuge. With Matthew's Nativity account, Egypt again becomes a place of refuge.

Exodus talks about frightened parents, in the Diaspora, who are unwelcome and unsafe and enslaved. Matthew recounts how Mary and Joseph have to flee to Egypt. Even Luke talks about family displacement when Joseph and Mary travel from

Nazareth in Galilee to Bethlehem in Judea in order to register for the census ordered by Caesar Augustus. The families are on the road, vulnerable.

Connections between Moses and Jesus continue, as do connections between other Old Testament stories and those in the New. Jesus would have known those Old Testament stories. Did he think of himself as a new Moses, seeing his people suffering under Roman rule? Did he see himself as a rescued child and thus felt himself called to a special role of protecting others? Did Mary think of herself in relation to that earlier Mary, Miriam, who worked with other women to save a child? Or did she think of herself as Jochebed, the mother who realizes that to save her son, she needs to let him go? Connections upon connections.

CHAPTER 1

The Conception and Birth of Isaac and Ishmael

The people Genesis depicts are not designed to be role models. To the contrary, we should struggle with our assessment of them: What would we do if we were in their sandals? With whom should our loyalties lie: natal family or nation? spouse? children? God? ourselves? Can we like, even admire, a person and still recognize that person's flaws? The answers are neither clear nor easy, but conversation around such questions has the potential to give us new insights into our own place in the world, our neighbors, and the God into whom the Bible offers glimpses.

Promises, Promises

The story of Abraham, his wives, and his children runs primarily from Genesis 11:26 to Genesis 21:43. It is then picked up in numerous places throughout both Old Testament and New. Prior to Abraham's introduction, the Bible gives what might be called primeval history: the creation of the world, with everyone in the divine image and likeness; the creation of Adam from dirt and Eve from bone, their disobedience regarding the forbidden fruit and their descent/ascent into civilization;

1

the first murder, when Cain kills Abel, which shows that to kill one person is to kill one quarter of the world's population; the relationship between the "sons of God" (or, in later tradition, fallen angels) and human women that produces the evils of the generation of the Flood; Noah's ark, the postdiluvian mistakes of Noah and his family, and the tower of Babel. From that glorious Creation narrative in Genesis 1 and the harmony of all of creation in Genesis 2, it's been tough going.

Many of these themes repeat: the wife (Eve) who tells the husband (Adam) what to do, even if that action creates problems; rival brothers; angels involved with conception and birth; imperfect families; dispersion from one's home to a new location. Each thematic repetition sends us back to the original, where we may see something new. Or, recognizing the repetition, we can ask ourselves if the second iteration, or the third, is an improvement or a regression. And in each repetition, we may find something of our own story.

In Genesis 12, Abraham provides the chance for God, and for readers, to restart following the mess at the Tower of Babel. God has scattered the people from Babel (i.e., Babylon, the later place of exile) over the face of all the earth (Genesis 11:8). From this geographical diversity—ironically fulfilling the Bible's first commandment, Genesis 1:28: "Be fruitful and multiply and fill the earth"—God zeroes in on one person. The Bible frequently moves from the universal (e.g., all Egypt) to the particular (e.g., two midwives, Pharaoh's daughter), and in doing so shows that one person's actions can have repercussions for all.

Naming

Abraham himself gets a do-over. "Abram," as he is introduced, starts over with a new identity and a new name. God, establishing a covenant, tells him, "No longer shall your name be Abram [the Hebrew means something like 'exalted (*ram*) ancestor or father (*ab*)], but your name shall be Abraham [*ab* is still 'ancestor' or 'father'; *raham* suggests a multitude], for I have made you the ancestor of a multitude of nations" (Genesis 17:5). For our purposes, we'll call him "Abraham" throughout.

Language nerds (I am one) find here a connection to Jesus, who refers to God as *Abba* (Mark 14:36; also Romans 8:15; Galatians 4:6), from that same *ab* root in both Hebrew and Aramaic. Fathers take various forms: heavenly, biological, adoptive, religious (as in the ecclesial title), political (father of the country), a (male) dissertation advisor is a *Doktorvater*. Abraham is not an ideal father (no figure in the Old Testament is); the text is not inclined to deify its figures but to depict them as flawed beings from whom we can learn, with whom we can empathize, or against whom we can rail. But he already raises questions of what we want in a father, and how fathers want to act and to be remembered.

Abraham's wife also experiences changes. She is named Sarai, which likely comes from the Hebrew root meaning "to rule." As part of the covenant, "God said to Abraham, 'As for Sarai your wife, you shall not call her Sarai, but Sarah shall be her name'" (Genesis 17:15). The new name means "princess." Although I like the name Sarah (Sarah, our daughter, was named after my father, Saul), I was not initially thrilled with its etymology. For a little girl to be called "princess" is one thing; for a ninety-year-old woman it strikes me as infantilizing. That is, until I read this story in light of the Moses story, and I realized that the first "princess" we meet is Pharaoh's daughter, the one who rescues Moses. So I wonder: Did Pharaoh's daughter have children of her own? Was she like Sarah? Our Sarah in Genesis plans to provide Abraham an heir by having Abraham conceive a child with her enslaved Egyptian, Hagar. Did Pharaoh's daughter provide herself a child by taking a son away from the enslaved Hebrew woman Jochebed?

Leaving Home

God tells Abraham, "Go from your country and your kindred and your father's house to the land that I will show you" (Genesis 12:1). Abraham obeys, and thus becomes, like Adam and Eve expelled east of Eden and Cain expelled east of east of Eden, trying to find a home away from home. Like Moses and many others, Abraham becomes another "stranger in a strange land" (Exodus 2:22; 18:3 KJV).

The irony here is that when God issued the command, Abraham had already left his land. Back in Genesis 11:31, we learn that Terah took his son Abraham as well as his grandson (Abraham's nephew) Lot, and Sarah the daughter-in-law from Ur of the Chaldees to go to Canaan, but they stopped at the city of Haran. There Terah dies. Abraham is introduced in mid-journey: already removed from his place of birth, but not yet at the place his father sought to go. I am reminded of Moses, who leaves Egypt, but never himself enters the Promised Land. I am reminded of Samson, blinded and brought in bronze shackles "down to Gaza" (yes, that Gaza), where he will die in the temple of the Philistine god. And I am reminded of the Nativity stories. In Matthew 2, Joseph brings his family from Bethlehem in Judea to Egypt for refuge and then returns from Egypt not to Judea, but to a small town in the Galilee called Nazareth. In Luke's account, Joseph and Mary go back and forth between Nazareth in Galilee and Judea: from Nazareth to Bethlehem to be registered for the census, then to Jerusalem to present Jesus at the Temple, then back to Jerusalem for pilgrimage festivals.

The biblical story is one of displacement, of refugees and migrants, people uprooted by famine, and people uprooted by empires. It is also a story of pilgrimage, of making connections with relatives who live in different locations, and of exploration. It is a story of people trying to find, and to make, a home.

Abraham's story, and so Jesus's story, asks us how we understand "home." Do we live where we were born, and if so, are we where we want to be? Did we set out for adventure or for a job; did we follow a loved one, or did that loved one follow us? Were we moved against our will? Did we move in order to make life better for ourselves and our families, or were we forced to move by war, economics, bigotry? Are we where we want to be, or where we think we should be? All this, and more from one verse.

In the next two verses, God promises Abraham that he will make from him a "great nation"; not only will God bless

5

Abraham, God will bless those who bless Abraham, so that in him "all the families of the earth shall be blessed." Thus this call, while it settles on one family rather than all of humanity, opens up to all humanity. The Old Testament is not just about one family or one nation, it is about how one person, one family, or one nation takes its place in the global setting.

To be a "great nation" requires others; one cannot be a great nation on one's own, no matter how high the ego. But Abraham is already a senior citizen, as is his wife Sarah, and so far, no children. Genesis 11:30, after introducing Sarah, makes the point, she "was barren; she had no child." This introduction bothers me. Yes, Sarah's infertility is necessary to the plot, but surely there is more to say about her.

Then again, biblical mentions of infertile couples are as good as a positive pregnancy test. But Sarah must wait. The family arrives in Canaan, the Promised Land, in Genesis 12:5. In Genesis 12:10, we learn of a local famine, so our protagonists hit the road again. Abraham takes Sarah and decamps to Egypt, which, because it relies on the annual flooding of the Nile rather than on rainfall, functions as the local breadbasket. In three generations, the first Joseph, the son of Jacob, again relocates his family to Egypt when another famine hits Canaan. That is how, generations later, Moses happened to be born in Egypt.

In Egypt, Abraham speaks his first words to Sarah, "I know well that you are a woman beautiful in appearance..." (Genesis 12:11). This is not necessarily an auspicious start. If this is the first thing I hear in the morning, I fear the next comment is going to be a request to pick up the dry cleaning.

Abraham then explains his fear that Pharaoh (another one, also unnamed) will have him killed and claim Sarah for his own. Therefore, she should pretend she is his sister, so that "it may go well with me because of you and that my life may be spared on your account" (Genesis 12:13). Sarah complies, the Egyptians remark on her beauty, praise her to Pharaoh, who then, on cue, takes Sarah into his household. The goal was not to play canasta. Pharaoh rewards Abraham with gifts, including enslaved females (perhaps explaining how Hagar entered the household). A plague ensues (foreshadowing the Exodus story). Pharaoh, realizing that Sarah is the cause, evicts her and Abraham from Egypt. Likely Hagar accompanied them.

Hagar's Pregnancy

Back in Canaan, after numerous adventures and another decade of infertility, Sarah recognizes Abraham's yearning for a child (actually a son; the setting is the patriarchal Late Bronze Age). Convinced that she, at age ninety, was unlikely to conceive, Sarah places Hagar in Abraham's bed; the goal is for Hagar to have a child whom Sarah would then claim as her own. The Bible describes, "Now Sarai, Abram's wife, bore him no children. She had an Egyptian slave whose name was Hagar, and Sarai said to Abram, 'You see that the LORD has prevented me from bearing children; go in to my slave; it may be that I shall obtain children by her.' And Abram listened to the voice of Sarai" (Genesis 16:1-2). Whether Hagar found this situation intolerable or as a move for social advancement goes unstated.

7

In the Bible, stories don't repeat; they rhyme. That first unnamed Pharaoh in Genesis 12 took Sarah into his household and so enslaved her with the unstated goal of having intimate relations with her. In Genesis 16, Sarah does the same thing: she puts Hagar into Abraham's bed, just as Abraham was willing to put her into Pharaoh's bed. Generations later, the Egyptians did to the Israelites in effect what Sarah did to Hagar: enslavement followed by both physical and psychological oppression. Trauma repeats through the family, and through the years.

Things do not work out the way Sarah planned. Hagar gets pregnant, and now we begin to see things from her perspective. The NRSVue flaccidly states, "And when she saw that she had conceived, she looked with contempt on her mistress." The Hebrew puns by saying, "The great lady [the Hebrew can also mean "female ruler"] became light in her eyes" (Genesis 16:4). The expression "lightweight" fits. Not only does Hagar look down upon Sarah as infertile, as the pregnant Hagar gains weight, Sarah looks lighter in comparison.

Sarah, furious, abuses Hagar, an early reference to domestic abuse. More, she complains to Abraham: "I gave my [enslaved woman] to your embrace [the Hebrew means "bosom," not embrace; I think the translators have a problem with the word "bosom"; we are speaking about intimate relationships], and when she saw that she had conceived, she looked on me with contempt [literally, 'I became light in her eyes']. May the LORD judge between you and me!" (Genesis 16:5). Sarah wants Abraham to do something. In her view, the enslaved should be not only obedient but also subservient. They should "know their station."

Sarah's reaction is also a warning. Her rejection of Hagar, to whom she never speaks, shows that assertions of power or dignity by people in subordinated situations can have negative repercussions. Talk back to the CEO and one's job can be in danger. Talk back to the professor and one's grades may suffer. Talk back to law enforcement, and one might be handcuffed, or killed. In Hagar's case, we may take the message that while dignity and agency are to be desired, gloating is not the best form of subversive freedom.

Abraham refuses to intervene. He observes, "Your slave is in your power [literally, 'in your hand']; do to her as you please [literally, 'what seems good in your eyes']" (Genesis 16:6a). I find this comment highly problematic. The literal reading "in your hands" makes a visceral impression: It may be by Sarah's hand that Hagar is struck or whipped. First we see through Hagar's eyes that Sarah became "light"; now we see through Sarah's eyes the possibilities of abuse. Hagar is pregnant with Abraham's child, and he doesn't appear to care about either her or the baby. Nor does he care about Sarah: he offers no word of love or comfort. His coldness anticipates the coldness of the Egyptians who, as we have seen, find no compunction against killing infants. This text, and verse, require discussion.

Hagar is enslaved to Sarah, and her status is reaffirmed by everyone from Abraham to Sarah to an angel Hagar encounters, even by Hagar herself. Genesis 16:1 introduces her as Sarah's property: Sarah "had an Egyptian slave whose name was Hagar." In the next verse, Sarah tells Abraham to "Go in to my slave; it may be that I shall obtain children by her." Genesis 16:3 explains that Sarah "Took Hagar the Egyptian, her slave, and gave her to Abram as a wife." In 16:5, Sarah complains to Abraham, "I gave my slave to your embrace…"

The narrative then returns to Hagar's enslaved status. Genesis 16:6b (NRSVue) states "Then Sarai dealt harshly with her, and she ran away from her." The Hebrew verb underlying "dealt harshly" comes from the term *oni*, meaning to abuse, afflict, oppress, humiliate. The noun *oni* shows up in other occasions where God responds to desperate situations. In the Moses story, Exodus 3:7 offers, "Then the LORD said, 'I have observed the misery [*oni*] of my people who are in Egypt; I have heard their cry on account of their taskmasters. Indeed, I know their sufferings." Hagar, the Egyptian slave who suffered under Sarah's hand, finds connections to the Israelites who suffer under the hands of the Egyptians. No group is innocent of oppression; no group fails to have experienced oppression.

The term *oni* also has economic implications. When God pays attention to suffering and condemns abusive practices, the focus can also concern poverty and attendant social issues: food and housing instability, vulnerability, often despair. On occasion, the term *oni* is paired with *gēr*, "not native born" (as in Moses's son, *Gēr-shom*, "stranger there"). Leviticus 19:10 insists, "You shall not strip your vineyard bare or gather the fallen grapes of your vineyard; you shall leave them for the poor [*oni*] and the alien [*gēr*]." We'll return to the term *oni* in chapter 4, where we find its Greek translation in Mary's Magnificat.

The Bible does not hide social sins: sex trafficking, murder, incest, abuse of weaker members of the household, the ignoring of abuse by people who could step in (here, Abraham). The Bible tells these stories not for reasons of prurience; it tells them so that victims can feel empowered to come forward; it tells them so that victims know that they are not alone. More, it tells them so that the perpetrators can face their own responsibilities and, ideally, seek forgiveness, attempt reconciliation, and make restitution when they can.

The Annunciation to Hagar

Hagar flees from Sarah's hand, and we readers, together with "the angel of the Lord," find her "by a spring of water in the wilderness, the spring on the way to Shur" (Genesis 16:7). The text sounds like a travel guide, as if the reader, map in hand, finds the spring on the Shur highway. Geographical notices are also intertextual resonances. The wilderness reappears where the Israelites spend forty years between slavery in Egypt and the entry into the Promised Land. Exodus 15:22 reports that "Moses ordered Israel to set out from the Red Sea, and they went into the wilderness of Shur. They went three days in the wilderness and found no water." We know from Genesis 16 that they will find water eventually. Fleeing from oppression, they are not the first, and they will not be the last.

It's a cliché to state that we have wilderness moments when we feel deserted (pun intended). But it is also in the desert, without the distractions of civilization, of quotidian duties, that we can feel closer to God, or we can better understand what we need to do or even who we are. When John the Baptizer called people from their homes to the wilderness, to reassess

11

their relationship to God, he knew what he was doing. When Jesus enters the wilderness to face temptation, he can remind us of Hagar in both being dependent on God for sustenance and in returning to a life of both joy and suffering.

The angel states, "Hagar, slave of Sarai, where have you come from and where are you going?" (Genesis 16:8). He knows, even reinforces, her identity. she is Hagar, Hebrew *ha-gar*, the "stranger" or "alien" or "immigrant." She is the outsider, in all manner of speaking, to Abraham's camp. More, she is enslaved. At the same time, this foreign, pregnant, "slave of Sarah" encounters the divine. This foreign woman is in the desert, where nationality is of limited or no value. She is enslaved, and yet she is not in the household that enslaved her. Her identity is changing in this wilderness moment.

Hagar responds, "I am running away from my mistress [female ruler] Sarai" (Genesis 16:8). Hagar misses the irony: that she was able to run suggests that Sarah's power is limited. More, Hagar answers the first part of the question, "Where have you come from?" But she has not answered fully: she has come *from Egypt*. She has come *from a house of slavery.* Nor does she answer the second part of his question at all, "Where are you going?" She cannot yet see herself as going *to freedom* or *to her own destiny* or even perhaps back *to Egypt*. Nor is she going alone, as she has to care not only for herself, but also for her unborn child.

I would like at this point for the angel to arrange an intervention. He could, with Hagar, return to Sarah and Abraham, encourage Sarah to apologize for mistreating Hagar, seek reconciliation, and then give Hagar the choice of where she wants to live. But, no. The angel orders Hagar not just to return, but to "return to your mistress, and submit to her" (Genesis 16:9). The Hebrew is more visceral, "Return to your woman ruler and be afflicted [*oni*] beneath her hand."

Excuses have been offered to explain this dreadful sentence. To claim that the angel is concerned about the baby, I'm not buying them. If God can provide manna and quail for the Israelites in the wilderness, God can provide for Hagar. To claim that the angel hopes for a reconciliation between Sarah and Hagar, or for Abraham's showing care for Hagar, I don't see this possibility. At least the Bible does not state that Sarah continued to abuse Hagar. It is possible that Hagar considers the angel's directive and now behaves in the subservient manner Sarah wants.

Yet following this instruction, the situation is no longer the same. Hagar has encountered an angel. Her story tells us that God sees us not just when we pray, but when we are too tired, too thirsty, too oppressed to pray.

Then comes the good news. The angel tells Hagar that her offspring will be so numerous that they cannot be counted (Genesis 16:10). The NRSVue offers, "I will so greatly multiply your offspring that they cannot be counted for multitude"; the Hebrew, again, is more emphatic: "multiplying I will multiply your seed that they cannot be counted for the multitude." This is the same promise God made to Abraham in Genesis 13:16 (cf. 15:5), "I will make your offspring like the dust of the earth, so that if one can count the dust of the earth, your offspring also can be counted." Hagar will not be the last of her generation; her children will be as numerous as those of Abraham and Sarah. It is not through her son that the biblical covenant continues, but that does not mean his story ended. Islam has different and more extensive stories of Ishmael, including the note that he was the direct ancestor of Muhammed.

The angel next tells her that the baby will be a boy (no surprise) and that she is to call him Ishmael (I can't help but think here of *Moby Dick*!). The name means "God hears"; the *sh-m-a* root is the same as we find in the call, "Hear [*shema*], O Israel, the LORD is our God, the LORD alone" (Deuteronomy 6:4). The Hebrew *el* means "God" as in El Elyon or El Shaddai. The angel explains the name: The child is to be called Ishmael because God has heard (NRSVue "has given heed") "to your affliction" (*oni*, Genesis 16:11). This is the affliction to which God pays heed. This is the affliction that needs to be redressed. God hears the cries of any afflicted person. We can image that, if God is just, redress will occur, somehow.

The angel continues: "He shall be a wild ass of a man, / with his hand against everyone, / and everyone's hand against him, / and he shall live at odds with all his kin" (Genesis 16:12). Okay, I'm not thrilled with this prediction. I would not appreciate someone telling me, when I was pregnant, "You'll have a wild ass." Better something like "He'll be a librarian" or "She'll be a hotel corporate sales executive." On the other hand, the prediction is one of complete freedom. Unlike his mother, Ishmael will not be enslaved, whether legally or socially. He will do what he wants, on his own terms.

Nor are such predictions necessary indications of one's fate. Genesis is not the Tragedy of Oedipus, predicted to kill his father and marry his mother, which despite the efforts of his parents to prevent this fate, is exactly what happens. Classics give us tragedies while the Bible is, in the formal classification of genre, more often a comedy in that differences are often reconciled and there is a happy ending of sorts. Ishmael is not fully as the angel describes him. According to Genesis 25:9, Isaac and Ishmael together bury their father Abraham in "the cave of Machpelah." Here Ishmael is hardly "at odds with all his kin" (Genesis 16:12).

The modification of the prediction sends us forward to Jesus. Gabriel tells Mary about her son: "He will be great and will be called the Son of the Most High, and the Lord God will give to him the throne of his ancestor David" (Luke 1:32). The prediction has yet to come fully to fruition. More important, missing here is the notice of Jesus's death. Gabriel provides Mary good news; it will be Simeon in Luke 2:35 who tells Mary that a sword will pierce her own soul. Predictions can be partial; they are not the full story.

Genesis 16 now turns from emphasizing hearing to a concern for seeing. In Genesis 16:13, Hagar "named the LORD who spoke to her, 'You are El-Roi,' for she said, 'Have I really seen God and remained alive after seeing him?" What a glorious verse! Hagar—the pregnant enslaved woman, taken from her home in Egypt, placed into Abraham's bed, and then abused by Sarah, becomes the first person in the Bible to name God. This is no ethnocentric text; it is one that opens revelation to any and all.

The angel tells Hagar what to name her son, but she names God. She calls God *El* (again, the generic word for "god") *Roi* (pronounced, according to the vowels later put into the Masoretic text, "Ro-ee," rhymes with "go see" rather than "coy" or "boy"). (Thoughts of the son in *The Jetsons* are permitted only for the sake of nostalgia.) The name means "God who sees" or "God sees." The question Hagar asks means something like "Have I really seen God and remained alive after seeing him?" It's a good question, given that in Exodus 33:20, God tells Moses, "You cannot see my face, for no one shall see me and live." That is, except when they do. Her Hebrew literally reads, "Is it also here that I have seen after he has seen me?" To know that we are seen, really seen, whether by God, or a friend, a lover, a student…changes our self-perception, whether for good or for ill. The point is not to think of God like Santa, who sees us when we're sleeping and knows when we're awake and is keeping a naughty-to-nice tally. The point is that we are noticed, and in that notice we are valued. By seeing and by being seen, Hagar's self-worth is heightened.

Hagar's naming is remembered. The narrator notes that the well where she encountered the angel was called "Beer-lahai-roi" – the "well [*beer*] of the living one" (*la-chai*, as in the Hebrew toast, *l'chaim*, "to life") who sees me (*ro-ee*). On the map, it's between Kadesh and Bered (Genesis 16:14), and Kadesh will figure in Israel's wilderness journey (see e.g., Numbers 20).

This part of the story ends with the notice that Hagar bore Abraham a son, and that Abraham named him Ishmael (Genesis 16:15). The narrator three times mentions that Hagar gave birth to the child: *"Hagar bore* Abram a son, and Abram named his son, whom *Hagar bore,* Ishmael. Abram was eighty-six years old when *Hagar bore* him Ishmael. "Hagar bore...Hagar bore...Hagar bore" (Genesis 16:15-16, emphasis added). She's doing all the work; she cannot be forgotten.

Finally, unless Abram had a chat with an angel that went unrecorded, Hagar told him what to name the boy. He listened to the voice of his wife, here his wife Hagar. God has heard.

The tag at the end is that when the baby was born, Abram was eighty-six years old. God bless him.

Isaac, the Occasion for Laughter

When Abraham was ninety-nine (by my math, this makes Ishmael thirteen), he and God have another chat. God repeats the promise that Abraham will be "the father [NRSVue "ancestor"] of a multitude of nations" (Genesis 17:4), changes Abram's name to Abraham, father of many (17:5), and states that he will be "exceedingly fruitful" (17:6). I wonder if Ishmael was listening. If Abraham is going to be the ancestor of a multitude, Ishmael will have a lot of work ahead.

God then promises Abraham and his descendants an eternal covenant (17:7) which includes all of Canaan. In turn, Abram is to circumcise himself (I can't imagine), and every male member (I've carefully phrased this point) of his household (17:10-13).

While Abraham is pondering this (were Ishmael listening, I suspect his initial delight at the idea of multiple offspring was dampened) message, God drops another bombshell: Sarah will bear a son. Given her menopausal status, "Abraham fell on his face and laughed and said to himself, 'Can a child be born to a man who is a hundred years old? Can Sarah, who is ninety years old, give birth?" (Genesis 17:17). I would have laughed too. This laughter, the idea that the unbelievable, the unthinkable, can be thought and believed—and more, can come true—is part of the biblical tradition. The laughter is joyful.

Birth stories of Ishmael, Isaac, Moses, Samson, Samuel, John, Jesus... prompt us to ask "What if?" The Bible invites us to open our imaginations, and to recover the innocence of childhood, when all things seem possible. I think of Mark 10:15, where Jesus tells his followers, "Whoever does not receive the kingdom of God as a little child will never enter it," and of Jesus calling his disciples "little children" (see John 13:33). Mustard seeds do not become giant trees, but to imagine that a small seed can turn into something magnificent may be what drives the next great invention or movement. Post-menopausal women do not give birth (I put myself in this category, and just as well), but age should not hinder the fertile mind.

Abraham, who is not convinced about Sarah's ability or, perhaps, also his, to participate in this project, reminds God that he already has a son: "O that Ishmael might live in your sight!" (Genesis 17:18). God reassures Abraham both that Sarah will give birth to a son who is to be named Isaac (the name comes from the Hebrew root meaning "to laugh") and that all will be well, really well, with Ishmael.

In the next scene, Abraham circumcises the thirteen-year-old Ishmael, and he has himself circumcised as well (Genesis 17:23-27), a scene that, as we will see in chapter 4, echoes in the circumcisions of John and of Jesus. The covenant has prevailed through thousands of years.

The Conception and Birth of Isaac

One never knows when visitors will bring astonishing news. When my Ring doorbell chimes, the announcement concerns someone taking the dogs out or in, delivery people (nice, but not earth-shattering), and the rare missionary who climbs up the driveway (always interesting). But to this point, no angel at the door has announced that I will become pregnant (at my age, God forbid). But the Bible opens the door to remarkable events.

According to Genesis 18:1, the LORD (Hebrew *YHWH*) appeared to Abraham, "as he sat at the entrance of his tent in the heat of the day." Abraham is resting. (Given the story of Hagar and the recognition of enslaved people in the household, we might wonder whether they had the same privilege of sitting in the tent rather than toiling in the fields.) Suddenly, Abraham looks up and sees three men. Perhaps he had been daydreaming, or napping, and missed their arrival. Perhaps they dropped down from heaven. Seeing them, he runs from the tent to meet them and "bowed down to the ground" (Genesis 18:2). Abraham has had supernatural encounters before. Bowing to the ground is what most people do with a theophany. On the other hand, I have always had the nagging thought that he was really happy for the company.

The theology here shows the impossibility of pinning this God down. First we hear that YHWH appeared; now we have "three men." For some Christians, the three represent the Trinity of Father, Son, and Holy Spirit. For Jews, traditionally, the three are God and two angels (the two angels will, in the next chapter, peel off and visit Abraham's nephew Lot in Sodom; it doesn't go well for Sodom). In the New Testament, Hebrews 13:2 uses the scene to encourage hospitality: "Do not neglect to show hospitality to strangers, for by doing that some have entertained angels without knowing it." The identity of the figures who visit Abraham remains just beyond our grasp. Something revelatory, supernatural, extraordinary, is about to happen.

We can contrast Abraham's reaction to that of Hagar, who upon encountering an angel/God/both, shows no fear. The angel speaks; she speaks back. Good for her. She also sets the scene for Mary, who upon meeting the angel Gabriel, does not prostrate herself. Luke only notes that upon hearing the angel's words, "Hail Mary," or, more accurately, "Greetings, favored one!" that "she was much perplexed by his words and pondered what sort of greeting this might be" (Luke 1:28-29). Divine greetings require interpretation.

Abraham then bustles with activity, or, better, he spends time telling other people what to do. Genesis lavishes attention on the details of his hospitality: He calls one of the visitors "my lord" (Hebrew: *adoni*; Greek: *kyrie*; the same term as *kyrios*, "lord," the title given to Jesus). Christians, reading the Septuagint, would come to see in the use of the term "Lord" (*kyrios*) a reference to Jesus. This is fabulous: reading Genesis 18 together with Luke 1, we have both the prediction by Gabriel that Mary will conceive and have a child and the prediction, in the Greek, by a figure later Christians identified as Jesus, telling Abraham and Sarah that they will have a child. Jesus *is* both the good news *and*, in Genesis 18, in retrospect, the deliverer of good news.

Back to Abraham: he tells the men to stay rather than to pass by, and he asks that water be brought so that the men can wash their feet (Genesis 18:4). Then Abraham offers "a little water" for their feet and "a little bread, that you may refresh yourselves, and after that you may pass on" (Genesis 18:4-5). One could take his comment as a less-than-subtle hint: stay for a snack, but don't plan on staying for dinner or spending the night. More likely, he is being modest.

When the men agree—they know that their host has more in mind than a quick snack—Abraham rushes (Hebrew: *mahar*) into the tent to Sarah and says, "Make ready quickly [same word, *mahar*: Sarah is to act as Abraham acted] three measures of choice flour, knead it, and make cakes" (Genesis 18:6). So much for "a little bread." Moreover, the biblical text suggests that Abraham had both servants and enslaved people to do this domestic work. By having Sarah prepare the cakes by her own hand, he is honoring his guests. (The chapter does not record what Sarah thought.)

The term "bread" appears 297 times in the Bible, and the numbers rise when we include references to "cakes" and "food" in general. Any text can provide insight into any other text (the technical term for this approach to reading is "intertextuality"). When we read our story of Abraham and Sarah in light of the Gospels, here are five of many more takeaways (takeouts?).

First, a little water for the feet reminds us of Luke 7 and John 12, where a woman (Mary the sister of Martha in John) anoints Jesus's feet at a meal, and especially of John 13, where Jesus washes the feet of the disciples in John's version of the Last Supper. Abraham establishes the model of serving others, and Jesus continues this model as an example of hospitality, discipleship, and service.

Second, Jesus will reuse those *three measures*. According to Matthew 13:33 (see also Luke 13:21), "He told them another parable: 'The kingdom of heaven is like yeast that a woman took and hid in [The NRSVue reads 'mixed in,' which is not what the Greek verb *krypto*, as in cryptology, means] three measures of flour until all of it was leavened'" (my translation). Reading Genesis in light of the Gospels, we find that Sarah's task is pregnant with meaning (I couldn't resist). Angelic messengers are sure signs that the kingdom of Heaven is breaking in, but so is any hospitality of generosity: When meals are shared the divine presence is welcome

Third, the kingdom of Heaven is about assessing time. In Genesis 18, Abraham rushes; Sarah rushes. There are moments we take our time and moments when we move with haste. The narrative slows down the action to describe the haste. It can prompt us to wonder about those moments when we take our time, and when we think, "Now." I am reminded of my own moments of hospitality (I'm a terrible cook, but I do have things on hand). Rather than spend time putting together the perfect antipasto or fruit salad, I'd rather rush through the food preparation and spend time with my guests.

Fourth, while Abraham speaks of "a little bread," three measures is about sixty pounds, more than enough to feed one husband and three angels (traditionally, as we'll see with Samson in chapter 2, angels do not eat). Abraham is abounding in generosity, which sends us to the Bible's other miraculous feedings, from the manna in the wilderness, to the prophet Elijah who orders the widow of Zarephath to "make me a little cake" and, when she does, despite her lack of resources during a drought, Elijah provides a "jar of meal [that] will not be emptied and a jug of oil [that] will not fail" until the rains come(1 Kings 17:8-14). Jesus alludes to this scene in his synagogue sermon in Luke 4:25-26. Upping the game, Elisha feeds one-hundred people, and even obtains leftovers, with only "twenty loaves of barley and fresh ears of grain" (2 Kings 4:42-44). These early meals also anticipate Jesus's feeding more than five thousand men, "besides women and children," in Matthew 14:13-21 (see also Mark 6:30-44; Luke 9:12-17; John 6:1-5—the only miracle story appearing in all four Gospels).

Fifth, the image of baking bread is also an image of pregnancy (as the crude expression "She has a bun in the oven" signals). Pregnancy is in the air.

Abraham then runs—at ninety-nine (good for him!)—to fetch a calf, gives it to a young man who rushed (*mahar*; there's a lot of *mahar*-ing going on) to prepare it (Genesis 18:7). The meal has become a team effort. I wonder if this young man (Hebrew: *na'ar*) is Ishmael, since in Genesis 21:12, following Sarah's order that Hagar and Ishmael be expelled, God tells Abraham, "Do not be distressed because of the young man [*na'ar*] and because of your [enslaved] woman...." Genesis 21:17, 18, 19, and 20 all refer to Ishmael as a young man (*na'ar*). And if he is Ishmael, we can only speculate as to how he would have reacted to the visitors' annunciation.

The hospitality scene ends in Genesis 18:8 when Abraham takes curds, milk, and the calf and sets the meal before the strangers; so much for just a "little water" and a "little bread."

Abraham stands under the tree while they eat. Eight verses about hospitality—this is overbaked, or overegged, but this passage is not over-easy. The story is supposed to be about conception, not about curds and calf.

Finally comes the prediction. The visitors begin by asking where Sarah is. I'd like to think that they wanted to thank her for the cakes. I'm also curious as to why they would ask: Don't they know? Or, were they checking to see if Abraham knew? To anticipate our chapter 2, the story of Samson's conception: Manoah does not initially know about his wife's encounter with an angel in the fields. To anticipate our chapter 3: It is not clear that Elkanah knows about Hannah's vow to God or conversation with the priest Eli. For chapter 4: It is not clear when or even if Mary told Joseph about Gabriel's visit. What secrets do we keep, and why?

Abraham informs the visitors that Sarah is in the tent. Were I writing this text, I would have had Abraham inviting her to join the gathering. The scene suggests the stereotypical 1950s household, with the women in the kitchen and the men outside, smoking cigars and talking about "important" matters.

One of the visitors announces that he will return when Sarah bears a son. Since "Abraham and Sarah were old, advanced in age" and "it had ceased to be with Sarah after the manner of women" (Genesis 18:11), Sarah—listening—burst out laughing. I'm delighted that she was listening. She did the baking; why should she be deprived of the conversation? I'm also delighted that the Bible mentions menopause, if delicately; what a great occasion to make a sermon relevant to probably half the members of the congregation. Finally, I'm delighted with Sarah's reaction. Not only does she laugh, which is a great thing because there is often very little to laugh about, she thinks about what this prediction means. The NRSVue has Sarah wonder, "After I have grown old, and my husband is old, shall I be fruitful?" This is not what the Hebrew says. In Hebrew, she asks, "My husband is old, shall I have pleasure?" The Hebrew term for "pleasure" is *edna*, a cognate of *Eden* (as in Garden of). Sarah is talking about the joy of conceiving. I remember this verse, Genesis 18:12, since it reminds me of Tchaikovsky's *1812 Overture*, with the cannons booming.

The Birth of Isaac

All goes according to prediction, although the narrator discreetly does not tell us about the conversation Abraham and Sarah must have had after the visitors departed. After several more adventures, including Abraham's pleading that God spare Sodom and Gomorrah should ten righteous people be found, and King Abimelech of Gerar's taking Sarah into his household just as an earlier Pharaoh had taken Sarah into his household, the prediction comes to fruition.

Genesis 21:1 states, "The LORD dealt with Sarah as he had said, and the LORD did for Sarah as he had promised." I'm not thrilled with this translation. "Dealt with" to me has a negative connotation: I have to deal with the leaky faucet or paperwork. The Hebrew offers the more poetic, "And YHWH visited [Hebrew *paqad*] Sarah as he said, and YHWH did for Sarah as he had spoken."

"Visited" suggests not leaky faucets but welcome guests; it suggests a house call. The Hebrew term can be neutral, negative, or positive. In Exodus 3:16, God from the burning bush commands Moses, "Assemble the elders of Israel and say to them, 'The Lord, the God of your ancestors, the God of Abraham, Isaac, and Jacob, has appeared to me, saying: I have given heed to you [literally, visiting, I have visited] and to what has been done to you in Egypt." Following Samuel's birth and then his mother Hannah's bringing the child to the priest at Shiloh, 1 Samuel 2:21 reads, "The Lord took note of Hannah; she conceived and bore three sons and two daughters." "Took note" is *paqad*, "visited."

Genesis 21 begins with a focus on Abraham, but it continually returns to Sarah. The second verse states, "Sarah conceived and bore Abraham a son in his old age." The next verse is repetitive, "Abraham gave the name Isaac to his son whom Sarah bore him" (Genesis 21:3). In a humorous sense, I suspect the author wants to make very clear both that Abraham is the father and that the child emerged from Sarah's body. Following the note that "Abraham circumcised his son Isaac when he was eight days old, as God had commanded him"—his son; yes, we've gotten the point—the narrator for a fourth and fifth time stresses Abraham's paternity: "Abraham was a hundred years old when *his son* Isaac was born *to him*" (Genesis 21:5, emphasis added).

In non-biblical sources from the ancient Near East, Greece, and Rome as well as in many other cultures, gods father children. Samson's father may well have been an angel, as we'll see in chapter 2. Early Jewish sources suggest divine paternity in the cases of Noah and Melchizedek.

Stories of divine paternity have also been read back into the story of the conception of Isaac. For example, the first-century CE Jewish philosopher Philo of Alexandria suggested that Isaac was not just in a metaphorical but also in a natural sense God's son. Further, in his Epistle to the Galatians, Paul offers an allegorical interpretation of conceptions and births of Ishmael and Isaac. He writes: "One, the child of the enslaved woman [i.e., Ishmael], was born according to the flesh; the other, the child of the free woman [i.e., Isaac], was born through the promise" (Galatians 4:23). The enslaved woman is Hagar; the free woman is Sarah. "Born according to the flesh" [Greek: *kata sarka*] suggests a physical relationship, and when Paul talks about "flesh" he means the human body. Our concern is the description of Isaac as having been "born through the promise." Perhaps Paul, like Philo, had some sense of Isaac's divine paternity.

Historians cannot resolve the question of how ancient readers, whether of Genesis or of Galatians, understood the practical matters of Isaac's conception and birth. Nor should we presume that all readers left the delivery room with the same interpretation. That a centenarian couple had a child should be miracle enough. We can take the point one more step: We can see that any conception and birth of a child who is wanted, a child who is loved, are sites of divine visitation.

The scene ends with Sarah saying, "God has brought laughter [Hebrew *tzechoq*, from the same root as "Isaac"] for me; everyone who hears will laugh [*tzechoq*] with me... Who would ever have said to Abraham that Sarah would nurse children? Yet I have borne him a son in his old age" (Genesis 21:6-7; the stress on her bearing a child echoes the earlier stress on Hagar's having done the same thing). I appreciate that Sarah notes that people will be laughing *with* her rather than *at* her. The laughter, that should continue through the generations, is not only the laughter that comes with the joy of a healthy baby and good experiences with lactation. Too often the elderly (I count myself among them) are laughed at when the subject comes to anything physical, let alone sexual. Apparently, sexual concerns for women are supposed to stop about the same time we become eligible for Social Security. The Bible is an earthy text, and its phrasing suggests that we are to think positively about senior sexuality. For those who might scoff at Sarah's motherhood in her advanced age, she takes the offensive. She will laugh first.

To anticipate the Nativity stories of Jesus, there is joy in good news, in hospitality, in childbirth, and even in the act of conception. There is attention to women's bodies, virginal, pregnant, sterile, menopausal; more, there is attention to women's pain and to pleasure. The angels, commenting on the elderly couple's doubts about this future conception, ask, "Is anything too wonderful for the LORD?" (Genesis 18:14). There is much to laugh about, and much to ponder.

And then...

Ishmael and Isaac grow up. Sarah, jealous of Abraham's first son and perhaps jealous of Hagar as well, insists that the two be banished. Abraham loved Ishmael (the text does not comment on his view of Hagar, or hers of him), but God instructs him to listen to Sarah's voice. Abraham expels his son Ishmael and Ishmael's mother from their home and into the wilderness. Isaac remains at home with his mother.

In Genesis 22, the next chapter, God tests Abraham's loyalty by commanding him to kill Isaac, and Abraham is prepared to comply. When Abraham is about to kill Isaac, God recognizes Abraham's fidelity. The child is spared when an angel calls down from heaven in a different type of annunciation, this one an affirmation rather than a new prediction: "Because you have done this, and have not withheld your son, your only son, I will indeed bless you, and I will make your offspring as numerous as the stars of heaven and as the sand that is on the seashore. And your offspring shall possess the gate of their enemies, and by your offspring shall all the nations of the earth gain blessing for themselves, because you have obeyed my voice" (Genesis 22:15-18). The followers of Jesus, early on, saw in Genesis 22 a prediction of the cross.

On the other hand, after this event, God never again speaks to Abraham, and Isaac and Abraham never again speak to each other. More, immediately after Genesis 22, this test of Abraham, we read that Sarah dies. What was left that Abraham had to say to Sarah, before it was too late? What would Isaac have said to his mother, or she to him? What else do we need to say?

There is much more to say about Abraham and Sarah and Hagar, Ishmael and Isaac. But the seeds have been planted for stories to come: about moving from one place to another to find a home, about desperate acts of desperate people, about slavery and agency, about rivalries and status, divine appearances and human reactions, miraculous conceptions and, for readers, conceiving the miraculous.

CHAPTER 2

The Conception and Birth of Samson

Accounts of the conception and birth of Moses are replete with sacrifice and risk: of reproducing during enslavement, of a people's survival, of the courage to disregard immoral political policies, of the importance of teamwork, of the role of women. The conception and births of Ishmael and Isaac are stories of hope and pathos: Sarah's desire to provide a child for Abraham; Hagar's desire for her honor and her freedom. They are also stories of master and enslaved, abuse and protest, comedy and miracle. We now turn to the accounts of the conception and birth of Samson, which are stories of humor. For those who think of the Bible as a sober and somber text, Judges 13 is a laugh-out-loud story in which the divine enters the human realm to bring joy both to the people encountered in the text and to those of us who read it two millennia after it was written.

The Setting: The Book of Judges

Overall, Judges is not a happy story. It should have been. In the previous Book of Joshua, Israel enters the Promised Land under the careful hand of Moses's successor Joshua (yes, the "son of Nun" [Exodus 33:11 and another thirty-nine times], which can cause confusion: the dad's name is "Nun"). Not only have the walls of Jericho come tumbling down (that they were not standing at the time calls into question the historicity of the entire conquest narrative), but also the book ends on a relatively high note.

Joshua, the "servant [or slave] of the LORD," dies at the age of 110, and the people bury him (Joshua 24:29-30). The next verse states, "Israel served the LORD all the days of Joshua and all the days of the elders who outlived Joshua and had known all the work that the LORD did for Israel." Following the numerous complaints of the wilderness generation and that unfortunate incident with the Golden Calf, everything looks good in Canaan. Joshua 24:32 notes that the Israelites buried the bones of Joseph, which they had carried up from Egypt, in Shechem. The book's last line is the notice that "Eleazar son of Aaron [the high priest, the brother of Moses] died, and they buried him at Gibeah, the town of his son Phinehas, which had been given to him in the hill country of Ephraim" (Joshua 24:33). All seems well in Israel.

Except these references to death and burial prove ominous. Joseph, Joshua, Eleazar—all dead. References to the hill country of Ephraim and to Gibeah return at the end of Judges in the disturbing story of the death of the Levite's concubine and the ensuing civil war. The new generation experienced neither slavery in Egypt nor the stress, and refining, of the wilderness. As the Exodus story begins, "Now a new king arose over Egypt who did not know Joseph" (Exodus 1:8), so this new generation of the period of the Judges does not remember its past.

Judges is a book that spirals downward. While the book of Joshua highlights Israel's military skill (likely a later reflection, created by the exilic community in Babylon who wanted to project images of past glory to help them deal with present displacement; the archaeological evidence does not support a conquest narrative), the Book of Judges highlights the people's infidelity. Just as the earlier narratives produce various conventions or type scenes of infertile wives, annunciations, endangered children, active women, etc., so Judges is one giant type scene marked by variations on the basic story: Israel sins; God delivers them into the hands of their enemies; a judge arises to defeat the enemies; the people live in peace; repeat. The first several judges, each with distinct personalities and talents, bring about temporary peace. Among them are Ehud the left-handed trickster, Deborah the military leader, Gideon (he of the hotel Bibles), and Jephthah the tragic hero.

Judges 13–16, the Samson Saga, comes near the end of the Book of Judges. Samson is the last judge, after which the chaos ensues. By the end of the book, there are no more judges, and there is no more peace. Rather than facing destruction by external military power, the people almost destroy themselves. The refrain, "In those days there was no king in Israel; all the people did what was right in their own eyes" (Judges 17:6; repeated with variants in 18:1; 19:1; 21:25) sets up 1 Samuel, which justifies the anointing first of Saul and then of David.

Given all this, that Judges 13 can find humor shows resilience of spirit. It also shows how humor can help respond to tragedy. If we forget how to laugh, we may well forget how to live.

Judges 13:1 begins, conventionally, "The Israelites again did what was evil in the sight of the LORD, and the LORD gave them into the hands of the Philistines forty years." We have gone from the God who sees the oppressed Hagar to the God who sees the evil that the Israelites do. Hagar's suffering is redressed; this evil must be addressed. Of the book's downhill motion, this opening provides the farthest slide, since forty years is the longest any of the tribes in the book had been subjugated. Forty years signals a generation. The impression is that this time, after rounds and rounds of sin, God has had it with these people. And yet, the covenant with Abraham and so with his posterity endures.

There is also a surprise in this opening, a break in the expected pattern. The author gives no indication that the people have repented. For example, according to Judges 10:10, the "Israelites cried to the LORD, saying, 'We have sinned against you, because we have abandoned our God and have served the Baals.'" These "baals" are manifestations of a Canaanite god whom the Philistines also worshipped and to whom temples were built in various locations. His name is familiar today from the parody in 2 Kings 1:2-3, which calls him Baal-Zebub, "lord (baal) of the flies" (Hebrew *zvuv*, an excellent example of onomatopoeia). The god's actual name was probably Baal-Zebul, "Lord of the prince."

The origins of the Philistines are not entirely clear, but archaeological and linguistic evidence, especially from Egypt, suggests they originated from Greek areas around the Aegean and the eastern Mediterranean. They settled on the Canaanite seacoast in the twelfth century BCE; their cities, including Ashkelon, Ashdod, Ekron, and Gaza, remain on maps today. The Bible describes military encounters between the Philistines and both King Saul and King David (the famous Goliath whom David kills with a slingshot is a Philistine). For our purposes, the Philistines are the "bad guys." The Philistines' own story is lost to history.

The Danites in Zorah

Judges 13:2 begins Samson's story: "There was a certain man of Zorah, of the tribe of the Danites, whose name was Manoah. His wife was barren, having borne no children." This opening doesn't sound promising if we listen with ancient Near Eastern ears, or at least with ears attuned to what else the Bible tells us about geographical markers.

Zorah shows up again in Judges 18. The chapter starts with what will become a refrain in the book's last three chapters: "In those days there was no king in Israel..." (Judges 18:1a). The refrain, which sounded back in Judges 17:6 after Samson's death, is typically followed by the line, "all the people did what was right in their own eyes." The refrain appears again in 19:1 and 21:25. It suggests that without a king, including a centralized government, funding (gained by taxation), and a military, chaos will reign. It is up to us to determine the truth of this statement: would we prefer empire or chaos? What is it that prevents people from doing what is right in *their own eyes*, and prods us to do what our neighbors think is right?

The refrain also has implications for Samson, since the Philistines will gouge out his eyes (Judges 16:21). When he

35

topples the temple in which the Philistines have bound him, and kills numerous Philistines as well as himself in the process, he prays, "Lord GOD, remember me and strengthen me only this once, O God, so that with this one act of revenge I may pay back the Philistines for my two eyes" (Judges 16:28). Whether this action, right in *his* eyes, would be right in the eyes of the reader (what if there were ten righteous people in the Philistine temple?) is another question.

Judges 18:1b reads, "In those days the tribe of the Danites was seeking for itself a territory to live in, for until then no territory among the tribes of Israel had been allotted to them." No explanation for this lack of allotment occurs. Despite Samson's success in breaking the power of the Philistines, the other tribes have not made common cause with Samson's tribe. Judges 18:2 notes that "the Danites sent five valiant men from the whole number of their clan, from Zorah and from Eshtaol, to spy out the land and to explore it." The previous valiant man of Zorah, of the tribe of Dan, was Samson. But instead of the end of his judging bringing peace, it brings apostasy.

Finding new land, the "Danites set up the idol [they had obtained in their journey] for themselves. Jonathan son of Gershom son of Moses and his sons were priests to the tribe of the Danites until the time the land went into captivity" (Judges 18:30). The captivity refers to the Assyrian conquest of the Northern Kingdom of Israel in 722 BCE, a captivity that gave rise to the legend of the ten lost tribes.

More problematic is the notice of their priests. Moses— yes, *that* Moses—had a son whom he named "Gershom"

(Exodus 2:22). As a reminder: the name, which refers to Moses's sojourn in Midian, comes from the Hebrew *gēr*, not-native-born (part of Hagar's name as well) and *shom*, meaning "there." Moses explains the name, famously in the King James Version (KJV) as "I have been a stranger in a strange land." Things have gotten so bad that Moses's grandson, and his children, promote idolatry. No lineage is safe; not all children follow in their parents' footsteps. Other readings of this verse suggest that the priest's father was a fellow named Manasseh; most likely this change was made to preserve Moses's reputation. Spin control is not a new invention.

Here are three other points concerning Samson's tribe, the tribe of Dan. First, in the Song of Deborah, likely one of the Bible's earliest passages, Deborah the judge talks about the tribes who joined her in battle, and those who did not. In Judges 5:17 she asks, "and Dan, why did he abide with the ships?" The verse suggests that the Danites may have been originally seafaring people, like the Philistines, and not initially connected to the group that made the Exodus from Egypt. Some scholars find their origins with a group known as the "Denyen" or the "Danuna," Greeks, perhaps mercenaries on the Egyptian payroll who were to keep the peace in the parts of Israel under Egyptian control in the twelfth and eleventh centuries BCE. Since we're veering here away from biblical studies and into "in search of ancient mysteries," I'll end this section with the note that ancestry is itself fluid. People conquer other peoples, populations migrate from place to place, and the various genetic genealogy services show that many of us are comprised of multiple ethnic groups.

Second, the author of the Book of Revelation, John, claims that he "heard the number of those who were sealed [for protection], one hundred forty-four thousand, sealed out of every tribe of the people of Israel" (Revelation 7:4). The list of the twelve tribes that follows omits the tribe of Dan. Consequently, Christian writers such as Irenaeus, writing in Lyon in the early second century, claimed that the antichrist will descend from the tribe of Dan. I do wonder: How today would one know?

On a third, less ominous note, from the Middle Ages on, claims were made that the Danes, the people of Denmark, descended from the Danites. Conversely, the Beta Israel, a group of Ethiopian Jews, also claims to be descended from the Danites. I'm a biblical scholar, not a geneticist, so I'll stop here with what we can conclude from this brief geographical survey: membership in the tribe of Dan is potentially problematic; Samson's death does not bring political relief to the Israelites, but it marks the moment when Israel's problems are more internal than external: Instead of being attacked by others, they will attack each other. In retrospect, the time of Samson will seem like the "good old days"; in the prospectus, the death of Samson and its aftermath set up the need for the monarchy: dynastic succession rather than charismatic leadership; centralized government rather than occasional tribal unity.

Manoah and His Wife

Finally, we have our focus, a Danite man named Manoah. His name, which comes from the same root as the name Noah (the fellow from the Flood), means "rest" in the sense of "relax" or "cease from work" (rather than "the rest of the story"). Noah starts out well, but in Genesis 9 he winds up getting drunk, which leads to some highly problematic events. Thus, with this intertextual reference, we are already primed: Will this man of Zorah bring rest, or drunken destruction, or both?

The Bible does not name Manoah's wife, but it does give physical details: "His wife was barren, having borne no children" (Judges 13:2). Recollections flood in: We are introduced to Sarah with the line, "Now Sarai was barren; she had no child" (Genesis 11:30). The verse can function as a tautology (tautologies are repetitive expressions, like "illegal trafficking" or "convicted felon," and here I am not overexaggerating), since "barren" seems synonymous with "having borne no children." However, the verse may be assigning the infertility to the wife, not to the husband. I've read ahead, and from what I know of Manoah, he would not be my first pick for the father of my child. The same word combination appears in Luke 1:7, which describes Zechariah and Elizabeth, the parents of John the Baptizer, as "they had no children because Elizabeth was barren, and both were getting on in years."

The notice of infertility also cues the type scene or convention, so already I am expecting a lunch, an angel to make an announcement, and a son.

Compared to the previous examples of this convention—Abraham and Sarah, Isaac and Rebekah, Jacob and Rachel—we know very little about these parents in Judges 13. The earlier narratives name the women. Here, nothing. The earlier narratives start with details about the families, including in each case prayers for children. Here, nothing. Manoah and his wife may be a happily married couple more interested in matters other than children. She may be wary of pregnancy and childbirth given the high mortality rates for childbirth. She may not be thrilled with Manoah.

It is sometimes helpful to imagine how we would cast a story (back to Victor Mature); visualizing a text can help with interpretation. For movie buffs, in the 2018 version of the Samson story, starring Taylor James (not to be confused with James Taylor) as Samson, Manoah is played by Rutger Hauer (*Soldier of Orange, Blade Runner*) and his wife, named Zealphonis, is played by Lindsay Wagner (*The Bionic Woman*). Manoah strikes me as miscast; but casting the Bionic Woman as his wife is a stroke of genius.

The Wife and the Angel

As if on cue, following the notice of infertility, the narrator reports, "And the angel of the LORD appeared to the woman and said to her, 'Although you are barren, having borne no children . . .'" (Judges 13:3a). We didn't need the repetition; neither did she. The angel is not telling the woman something she does not herself know. Then again, the repetition here sets up something miraculous. The next phrase is "'you shall conceive and bear a son'" (Judges 13:3b). Hang on to this phrase for a minute as we stop for the angel's prenatal instructions.

The angel continues, "Now be careful not to drink wine or strong drink, or to eat anything unclean" (Judges 13:4). This is excellent prenatal advice, and it dates well before knowledge of fetal alcohol syndrome. The avoidance of wine also sends us back to Noah (speaking of bringing "rest"), who was the first person both to plant a vineyard and to suffer the effects of over-indulging. Noah had difficulty with his son Ham engaging in some form of disrespect (see Genesis 9:22), so perhaps there will be fraught relationship between the baby-to-be and Manoah.

Regarding unclean food: the angel hints that the woman was not particularly observant when it came to the dietary regulations. One does not need to be told to avoid pork or oysters if they are not normally, or even possibly, on the menu. The concern is for the food approved by the laws of Leviticus (for animals, only ruminants with cloven feet and meat that has been ritually slaughtered; for seafood, only fish with fins and scales, and so on).

Now the problematic material. According to the NRSVue, in both Judges 13:3 and 13:5, the angel gives Mrs. Manoah the same message, "You shall conceive and bear a son." A close reading of the Hebrew, however, reveals both tense changes and distinctions. Judges 13:3 clearly expects something in the future because the woman has not yet borne a son. But Judges 13:5 says not "you shall conceive" but "And look, you are pregnant." The same expression in Hebrew occurs in Genesis 16:11, where the angel says to the obviously pregnant Hagar, "Look, you are pregnant and you will bear a son." The Hebrew for "pregnant" in both cases is *harah*, the same participle used in the famous verse, Isaiah 7:14, where the prophet says to the king, "Look, the young woman is pregnant [*harah*], and she will bear a son, and she will call his name 'Immanuel.'" For Isaiah 7:14 in the

41

Hebrew, the woman's pregnancy, already underway, is itself not a divine-human conception, but the child will be a sign to King Ahaz of future divine action.

The upshot is that the same expression—"look, you are pregnant and you will give birth to a son"—is used in all three cases. If Hagar is already pregnant (no question) and if the woman in Isaiah 7:14 is already pregnant (more or less obvious in the Hebrew; less so in the Greek translation), then Mrs. Manoah is, at this point, pregnant. The text gives no notice that she had gone home, canoodled with her husband, and then returned to the field. Nope: first not pregnant; now pregnant. No wonder the angel advised, immediately, against alcohol consumption. The child is already in utero.

The irony is almost inconceivable: Isaiah, which says nothing about a virgin giving birth, becomes a prediction of the miraculous because of the Greek reading. Judges 13, which is not usually cited in the context of a miraculous birth, may recount one. However, Mrs. Manoah is not, as far as we know, a virgin.

The idea that an angel would impregnate a woman is not unknown to the biblical tradition. As the name Manoah reminds us of Noah, so the narrative in Judges 13 sends us back to the story of the Flood. According to Genesis 6:2, "The sons of God saw that [human women] were fair, and they took wives for themselves of all that they chose"; from these relationships come the mysterious Nephilim (the Hebrew *n-ph-l* connotes having fallen): "The Nephilim were on the earth in those days—and also afterward—when the sons of God went in to the daughters of humans, who bore children to them. These were the heroes that were of old, warriors of renown" (Genesis 6:4). Another connection of these Nephilim to Samson, who was enormous enough to grasp two pillars of the Philistine temple, is easier to spot in the King James Version. For Genesis 6:4, the King James offers, "There were giants in the earth in those days..." Numbers 13:33 notes that compared to the Nephilim, the Hebrews said, "We seemed like grasshoppers." The Hellenistic Jewish book of Wisdom, sometimes called the Wisdom of Solomon(14:6), agrees regarding the size of these Nephilim: "For even in the beginning, when arrogant giants were perishing, the hope of the world took refuge on a raft." Giants, children of angels, not peaceful...? Sounds like Samson to me.

Such divine-human hybrids were common in antiquity, both in the ancient Near East or in Greek culture. From the Near East comes the warrior Gilgamesh and his buddy, the very hairy and equally semi-divine Enkidu; from Greece come Theseus, Perseus, and especially Hercules, who bears a number of traits in common with Samson, from superhuman strength to a penchant for violence to a gigantic body and a taste for dangerous women. For those of you interested in archaeology, the mosaics recovered from the fifth-century CE synagogue in Huqoq in the Galilee depict a gigantic Samson.

As the introduction notes, some of my students become concerned when they realize that the Bible shares common storylines with non-biblical traditions. A few, positively, see the external texts as revealing hints of the truth of the Christian tradition and its antecedents. They see a similar connection in Acts 17:23, where Paul uses the altar "to an unknown god" to suggest that the people of Athens had already intuited the Christian gospel.

Other students, rejecting the idea that the authors of the Bible are influenced by the world around them, conclude that the Sumerians and the Greeks cribbed from the Jews. It's an interesting thought, and while I'd like to take, on behalf of the Jewish people, credit for all Sumerian, Egyptian, Greek, Carthaginian, Roman... literature, the history doesn't work.

That the Bible shares common motifs with non-biblical (pagan) sources should be a cause of curiosity and, ideally, rejoicing, rather than a reason to worry. Good stories are universal, not particular. Variations on the themes can tell us a lot about the aesthetics, and even the values, of the storytellers. For me, the biblical text becomes even more alive, even more impressive, when seen within its cultural context.

When it comes to miraculous birth stories closer to the time of Jesus, Jews recounted several. For example, the text known as *2 Enoch* describes the birth of the priest-king Melchizedek (see Genesis 14; Psalm 110, and the Epistle to the Hebrews) to Sopanim, the wife of Noah's brother Nir. Sopanim, elderly and infertile (what else?) suddenly finds herself pregnant. The child is not Nir's, since Nir is a priest and he keeps himself celibate to be always at the altar (ejaculation would render him ritually impure). Mortified by her condition, Sopanim hides herself. Nir, discovering the pregnancy, condemns her, and she drops dead. From her corpse, a toddler emerges. After forty days, the angel Michael brings the child, named "Melchizedek," to heaven. The next scene is that of Noah building the ark. Those who claim that accounts of miraculous births in Matthew and Luke are residues of pagan tradition do not know the Jewish backgrounds.

Back to Judges: now comes the angel's explanation for the prenatal dietary requirements, "No razor is to come on his head, for the boy shall be a nazirite to God from birth" (Judges 13:5a). I was initially surprised that the angel does not state that the *child* should never let alcohol cross his lips. Nazirites are known for three things: not cutting their hair, not consuming alcohol, and not coming into contact with corpses. Samson will be a Nazirite, but only partially. He drinks; he kills; and finally, he tells his lover Delilah, "A razor has never come upon my head, for I have been a nazirite to God from my mother's womb. If my head were shaved, then my strength would leave me; I would become weak and be like anyone else" (Judges 16:17). Delilah takes the cue, and a haircut ensues. On second thought, the angel was probably in the right. Parents can tell their children what they want from them. Children will do what they want. (We'll see in the next chapter how Samuel follows the terms of his mother's vow and remains dedicated to God.)

If we parents force our children to follow our wishes rather than their own, we do them no favors. Almost every year, when I would speak to students about their vocational goals, individuals in the ministerial track would say something like, "My father wants me to be a pastor" or "My undergraduate teachers thought I would be a good college professor." When

I then asked the follow-up, "What do *you* want to do?" the conversations became much more productive. We parents do the best we can with what we have. And if we find ourselves condemning Samson's behavior (he's not my favorite biblical character, although I like Mrs. Manoah, a lot), then we are engaging our own ethical sense.

The term "nazirite" comes from the Hebrew word for "separate." Numbers 6:1-21 describes the process of taking a vow to be a nazirite, an option open to both men and women. The NRSVue's translation of Numbers 6:2, "When either men or women make a special vow, the vow of a nazirite, to separate themselves to the Lord..." is a correct reading of the Hebrew and *not* a gender-inclusive adaptation. Nazirites, who are to "be holy" (Numbers 6:5, 8; see also Amos 2:11-12), but only for a temporary period, are to avoid wine and beer, grapes, haircuts, and corpses, even for the burials of immediate family members. When the period of the vow ends, they offer a sacrifice, then shave their heads, and burn the hair.

The hair, the public symbol of the nazirite, can be understood as untrimmed, or disheveled, or even wild. It indicates a rejection of regular society or, broadly, civilization. The anthropological term for a nazirite is someone in a "liminal" space. It marks not only Samson, but also Elijah: the NRSVue describes him as a "hairy man" (2 Kings 1:8).

Now we come full circle back to the angel's annunciation regarding Samson's nazirite status. I wonder: as this ancient story was told through the generations, could an original account of a semi-divine figure, known for his long and miraculous hair, have become in the retellings Hebraicized? Explaining the long hair as the result of a nazirite vow more firmly locates Samson in ancient Israel's tradition.

Finally, the angel tells the woman, "It is he who shall begin to deliver [the term translated "deliver" derives from the same Hebrew root as the names Joshua, Hosea, and Jesus, and the term *hosanna*] Israel from the hand of the Philistines" (Judges 13:5b). The message is also ominous: He will begin, but he will not complete the task. Were I Mrs. Manoah, I would have asked for details, and then, perhaps, reached for a saltine.

Manoah's Reaction

Rather than ask the angel for more details, or checked to see if her feet had started to swell, the woman "came and told her husband, 'A man of God came to me, and his appearance was like that of an angel of God, most awe-inspiring; I did not ask him where he came from, and he did not tell me his name'" (Judges 13:6). This is not the sort of thing that happens on a regular basis. I can imagine telling my husband, "An unbelievably gorgeous fellow came to me at the Farmer's Market, but I can't give you details." A husband might suspect something more was going on than a discussion of the price of eggs.

The woman's description offers much to consider. First, she describes the fellow as a "man of God" (Hebrew: *ish ha-elohim*), which suggests a godly person, not a divine one. For example, Deuteronomy 33:1 (cf. Joshua 14:6) describes Moses as "the man of God" (*ish ha-elohim*), and the same description applies to Samuel (1 Samuel 9:7-8, 10), whom we meet in the next chapter. In 1 Kings 17 (cf. 2 Kings 19), the widow of Zarephath (we remember her from Jesus's synagogue sermon in Luke 4) identifies Elijah the prophet as a "man of God." In 2 Kings 4:16, the Great Woman of Shunem calls Elisha the prophet, who had just announced her pregnancy, "man of God." Moses, Elijah, and Elisha are no schlumps, but nor are they angels.

Second, the wife glosses "man of God" with "and his appearance was like that of an angel of God, most awe-inspiring." It is not clear if Mrs. Manoah knows he is an angel, thinks he may be an angel, or is trying to put her husband at ease. But she does raise the question: How do we know an angel, a messenger of God, when we see one? Again, Hebrews 13:2 is helpful: "Do not neglect to show hospitality to strangers, for by doing that some have entertained angels without knowing it." Any visitor can be an angel (it can happen); open table fellowship, or just inviting a stranger (Hebrew *gēr*) to a meal can be revelatory. We might also think of Jesus with his two disciples on the road to Emmaus. They have no clue who he is, and they only recognize him—after they have invited him to join them for a meal—in the Eucharistic image of the breaking of bread (see Luke 24:29-32).

Third, we might wonder about the phrasing. Mrs. Manoah states that the angel "came to me." The Hebrew reads *ba 'el* (not to be confused with *Baal*), "came to me," which can be a polite way of describing, well, canoodling. For example, it appears in Genesis 30:3, when Rachel says to her husband Jacob, "Here is my maid Bilhah; *go in to her*, that she may bear upon my knees and that I too may have children through her" (emphasis added). Deuteronomy 22:13 reads, "Suppose a man marries a woman but after *going in to her* dislikes her…" (emphasis added). Judges 3:20 describes how the trickster judge "Ehud *came to* [King Eglon], while he was sitting alone in his cool roof chamber, and said, "I have a message from God for you"(emphasis added). Literally, Ehud "came in to him": the Hebrew sets up a seduction scene that the English translation misses. Ehud then "reached with his left hand, took the sword from his right thigh, and thrust it into [the king's] belly" (Judges 13:21). When do we have a euphemism, and when an innocent description? Does it matter that the Bible is occasionally bawdy, and if so, why?

On a more serious note, the story of the angel raises questions: Do we sense the divine presence in some more than others? Do we just ascribe divinity, or holiness, or trust, on the basis of someone's looks, or someone's behavior? Here the topic of charisma arises, something that leaders typically have that is to be taken seriously.

Before Manoah has the chance to ask a question, the wife continues, "But he said to me, 'You shall conceive and bear a son. So then, drink no wine or strong drink and eat nothing unclean, for the boy shall be a nazirite to God from birth to the day of his death'" (Judges 13:7). When a text repeats, the repetition can serve to emphasize, can function as humor, or can be a modification of an earlier verse. Here the third reason is in play. The wife adds to the prediction, "from birth *to the day of his death*" (emphasis added)—something the angel never mentioned. Mrs. Manoah both predicts her son's birth and foreshadows his death.

We hear her comments echoed by Hannah, Samuel's mother, who vows, "O LORD of hosts, if only you will look on the misery of your servant and remember me and not forget your servant but will give to your servant a male child, then I will set him *before you as a nazirite until the day of his death.* He shall drink neither wine nor intoxicants, and no razor shall touch his head" (1 Samuel 1:11, emphasis added). That phrase, "until the day of his death" puts a worrying note on the vow. The connections between Samson and Samuel promote speculation: Samson, uncontrollable, rules by might; Samuel, the one to anoint the first king, needs to find someone who has self-control and rules by justice. They ask us what we want in a leader, even as they warn us about our choices.

The connections also promote contrast: we know nothing about Jesus's hair, despite the famous 1940 "Head of Christ" painting by Warner Sallman. But we do know that he is by no means a nazirite. "The Son of Man came eating and drinking, and they say, 'Look, a glutton and a drunkard, a friend of tax collectors and sinners!' Yet wisdom is vindicated by her deeds" (Matthew 11:19; see also Luke 7:34). Nazirites separate themselves from others; Jesus brings others to him.

Manoah now prays, but in the variation on the scene, he doesn't ask for a son. Nor does he ask that God open his wife's womb (which would be redundant). Instead, he prays, "Let the man of God whom you sent come to us again and teach us what we are to do concerning the boy who will be born" (Judges 13:8). Mrs. Manoah had already explained the prenatal and postnatal care, so Manoah needs another reason to ask for "what we are to do concerning the boy." I think Manoah wants to be included in the heavenly commanded action: He asks that the angel come to *us*, teach *us*, and tell *us* what *we* are to do—he wants to be part of the boy's life. His comment makes me think of Joseph. Post-New Testament legends depict young Jesus working in his father's carpentry shop. It's a lovely image.

The Second Appearance

Judges 13:9 reports, "God listened to Manoah, and the angel of God came again to the woman as she sat in the field, but her husband Manoah was not with her." God listened to Manoah! He is part of the picture after all, although he may not realize it. Nor does he know initially that his prayer has been answered. The angel again appears only to Mrs. Manoah, who is sitting "in the field." In general, wives in the early Iron Age, the setting of Judges, would be involved in gardening, tending to domestic animals, baking, cooking and preserving food, weaving cloth and making clothes, cleaning, and so on. Sitting in the field does not suggest plowing or planting or reaping. I picture her weaving a grass basket, or feeling exhausted, or even day-dreaming about that fellow she just met. Conversely, Manoah, the man, should be in the field. Perhaps, as his name suggests, he is "resting." Or perhaps there are times when prayer is more important than daily work.

Seeing the angel, the woman "ran quickly and told her husband, 'The man who came to me the other day has appeared to me'" (Judges 13:10). All that running reminds me of Abraham and Sarah running to provide hospitality. If the scene were filmed as a movie, it should be done as a comedy. As far as the woman's words, the expression for "appeared" is "came to" (the same potential euphemism encountered at the angel's first appearance).

Manoah, perhaps missing the pun, "Got up and followed his wife" (Judges 13:11a). Commentators frequently note that the wife should follow the husband and so see the couple as confounding gender roles. On the other hand, Manoah cannot go ahead of his wife because he did not know where she met the angel. Sometimes following is practical. Again I think of Jesus. While "to follow" in Greek can function as a technical term for discipleship, it can also describe Jesus who "got up and followed" the desperate father seeking a healing for his daughter (Matthew 9:19). Both leading and following can be discipleship moments.

In the field, Manoah "came to the man and said to him, 'Are you the man who spoke to this woman?' And he said, 'I am'" (Judges 13:11b). The Hebrew behind "I am" is not the same as God's famous "I am" (Greek) or "I will be what I will be" (Hebrew) to Moses at the bush in Exodus 3:14. The Hebrew here just means "I" or "It is I." Manoah does not appear impressed with the man, whose "appearance," as his wife described, "was like that of an angel of God, most awe-inspiring."

Manoah then asks: "Now when your words come true [the Hebrew can also be read as a prayer, "May your words now come true"], what is to be the boy's rule of life; what is he to do?" (Judges 13:12). Manoah asks no question about the pregnancy, as if that is already a done deal. His focus is on the child's future. The Hebrew does not speak of a "rule of life"; it rather asks about the "judgment of the lad." The issue is not how the boy is to behave in terms of diet and drink, but how he is to be assessed or even what the divine judgment about him is to be.

The angel ducks both questions. In the Bible, and especially with Jesus, people answer the questions they want to answer. Turning attention from the child back to the woman, the angel explains that she should "give heed to all that I said to her" (Judges 13:13). Then he repeats the prenatal instructions. The wife is silent, and the husband is again omitted from the instructions. I am getting the impression that the wife is the major partner in this relationship, as Rebekah was to Isaac. More, for the Gospels, Joseph appears last when he seeks the twelve-year-old Jesus in the Temple (Luke 2:41-52). Mary likely had the major parental responsibilities for the teenage Jesus.

Following all this talk about what not to eat, Manoah invites the angel to dinner: "Allow us to detain you and prepare a kid for you" (Judges 13:15). Echoes of Abraham back in Genesis 18, with all that talk about an infertile wife conceiving and giving birth to a son! At least Manoah doesn't ask his wife to do the cooking. Because traditionally angels do not eat, the offer may be a test to see if the fellow is really an angel. Conversely, Manoah may be clueless.

Our text here has another echo, this one from earlier in the Book of Judges. The judge Gideon, not the swiftest judge on the block, meets an angel of the Lord (it can happen). The angel commissions Gideon to free Israel from the hand of the Midianites, but Gideon demurs: his tribe of Manasseh is the weakest of the tribes, and Gideon himself is the weakest of the weak. The angel reassures Gideon, who responds with a request for a sign (how much does he need?) and an offer of lunch. He asks the angel to wait (much as the angel waits for Mrs. Manoah to bring her husband to the field) while he goes into his house and prepares both a kid (anticipating Manoah) and unleavened cakes (recollecting Sarah). The angel advises Gideon to put meat and cake on a rock and then pour the broth in which the meat had cooked onto a rock. Gideon, who now asks no questions, obeys. The angel touches the tip of his staff to the food, and fire bursts out. Then the angel of the Lord vanishes. *Now* Gideon understands the man was an angel. No one eats lunch.

Following Gideon, we readers can anticipate another sacrifice and so another type scene. The angel hints, "If you detain me, I will not eat your food, but if you want to prepare a burnt offering, then offer it to the LORD" (Judges 13:16a). We readers know what is going on; so does Mrs. Manoah, but "Manoah did not know that he was the angel of the LORD" (Judges 13:16b). I can imagine this story being presented orally, with the audience calling out, "Manoah—he's an angel" or even "Manoah, you dunce, he's an angel." The audience will do the same thing with Samson, when Delilah asks him, several times, about the source of his strength—"Don't tell! Don't tell!"

Manoah tries again, as if hoping to keep the angel's company. He asks, "What is your name, so that we may honor you when your words come true?" (verse 17). Knowing someone's name conveys power: this is why Jesus asks the name of the demon who possessed the man in Gerasa; this is where the demon responds, "My name is Legion" (Mark 5:9). To this point in the Bible, we have no named angels. Michael and Gabriel appear in the (relatively late) Book of Daniel. The Book of Tobit in the Deuterocanonical literature features Raphael. In the earlier parts of the Bible, angels are interchangeable: they are unnamed, but they speak to Hagar and Abraham, Rebekah and Jacob, Moses and Gideon and Manoah.

And they speak for God. Nor does an angel need to be honored, for the honor should to be God.

The angel again refuses to answer the question. Instead, he poses his own: "Why do you ask my name? It is too wonderful" (Judges 13:18). That's it. There will be no control over him by Manoah or the wife. He remains mysterious, and gorgeous. More, the angel's namelessness reminds us of Mrs. Manoah, the wife and mother, whose name is also withheld. Even more, the notion of this "wonderful" name sends us back to Genesis 18:14, where Abraham's visitor asks, "Is anything too wonderful for the LORD? At the set time I will return to you, in due season, and Sarah shall have a son."

There being nothing left to say, Manoah makes the offering to the Lord "who works wonders" (Judges 13:19). The description is a play on the "too wonderful" name of the angel. The angel ascends to heaven in the sacrificial flame (Judges 13:20).

At this point, Manoah finally perceives, more or less. Watching the angel ascend (and not being burnt to a crisp), husband and wife fall on their faces (Manoah in fear and reverence; I wonder if the wife is laughing). The author notes, "The angel of the Lord did not appear again to Manoah and his wife"

(Judges 13:21a). We have no indication that either Manoah or Mrs. Manoah prayed for another appearance. "*Then*, Manoah realized that it was the angel of the Lord" (Judges 13:21b, emphasis added). *Then!* Manoah is not the swiftest Danite in the neighborhood.

Again, Manoah proves himself obtuse. He tells his wife, "We shall surely die, for we have seen God." He sounds like Gideon back in Judges 6:22, who after watching the angel ascend cries, "Help me, Lord GOD! For I have seen the angel of the LORD face to face." Somehow, biblical characters do not get the message that if an angel commissions them, they are not going to die, at least immediately. Angels do not waste their time. It doesn't take a PhD in theology to make this conclusion.

The wife, quicker on the uptake, explains (I cannot determine if her tone is patient or impatient): "If the LORD had meant to kill us, he would not have accepted a burnt offering and a grain offering at our hands or shown us all these things or announced to us such things as these" (Judges 13:23). The angel has departed; it is now up to husband and wife to ponder what they have heard, and to obey the instructions they have received.

The Birth

The chapter ends with the announcement that "The woman bore a son and named him Samson. The boy grew, and the LORD blessed him." After some time, "The spirit of the LORD began to stir him in Mahaneh-dan, between Zorah and Eshtaol" (Judges 13:24-25). While Mr. and Mrs. Manoah will appear later in the story, we leave them here to comment on the naming of the child.

The Bible notes that the name Ishmael, "God hears," relates to God hearing Hagar in the wilderness. Isaac was named "laughter" because Sarah, and Abraham, laughed at the notion that at their age they would have a child. Moses received his name when Pharaoh's daughter "drew him" out of the water. But there is no explanation given for the name Samson.

The Hebrew *shimson*, whence the English "Samson," is a cognate of the word *shemesh*, meaning "sun." This sun will be eclipsed by Delilah, whose name is a cognate for the Hebrew word for "night." Samson is strong and impressively large, but he is more dim bulb than light of the world. The name also adds to the sense that the biblical authors present him as a folkloric figure, both superhuman and flawed, endearing and violent, heroic and, at the end, tragic.

We leave Manoah and his wife with laughter before the tragedy, working together, with memories of angels and hopes of redemption. And we see parents who do the best for their child, even while Samson, perhaps channeling angelic genetics, will forge his own path.

CHAPTER 3

The Conception and Birth of Samuel

I had for decades pitied Hannah, the mother of Samuel. She is desperate to have a child. She is taunted by her frequently pregnant co-wife Peninnah. When she prays fervently for a baby, the priest Eli accuses her of being drunk. Finally a mother, she keeps the little boy only three years, and then delivers him into the care of Eli in fulfillment of a vow. She is like Sarah, unable to have a child; she is like Hagar, oppressed by a co-wife. Like Hagar, she lives in a place of abuse. Like Hagar, she is initially rejected by a man in authority.

Hannah's canonical placement makes her even more pathetic. Christian Bibles place the Book of Ruth between Judges and 1 Samuel. Ruth—another story about infertility of both women and land, couples on the road, an elderly husband, two women bound together, and pregnancy and childbirth—buffers the tragedy that is the end of Judges, "In those days there was no king in Israel; all the people did what was right in their own eyes" (Judges 21:25); the Hebrew is gender-specific: "A man did what was right in his own eyes"). After the happy story of Ruth, the ancestor of David (see Matthew 1:5), Christian Bibles lead into 1 Samuel.

In the Hebrew canon (the Tanakh), 1 Samuel immediately follows Judges, and the Book of Ruth is placed toward the end of the canon in the Ketuvim, the "Writings." When the story of Hannah is placed in immediate proximity to Judges, we see more tragedy. In Judges 11, the judge Jephthah—the child of a prostitute, rejected by his father and half-brothers until they seek his military prowess to help defeat the Ammonites—vows to God, "If you will surely give the children of Amon into my hand, it will be that the one who comes out of the doors of my house to meet me at my return in peace from the children of Amon, and will be to the Lord (YHWH) and I will cause to offer up a burnt offering" (Judges 11:30-31, my translation). The one to greet Jephthah is his daughter, his only child (suggesting that Jephthah hoped that he would be greeted by the family dog does not improve this story). Jephthah, offstage, fulfills his vows. Hannah, too, vows that, should she bear a son, she would dedicate him to God. She, too, fulfills her vow.

I have come to find Hannah much less pathetic, more complicated, and much more interesting. My approach is now less to pity her than to understand her.

This chapter focuses on 1 Samuel 1:1-20: The introduction of Elkanah and his two wives, the relationship between Hannah and Peninnah, a replay of the stories of Sarah and Hagar as well as Rachel and Leah; Hannah's relationship with her sympathetic husband; her visit to Shiloh and her prayer for a son; her conversation with Eli the priest, who provides the annunciation; her pregnancy, and the birth of Samuel. Readers should continue through 1 Samuel 2 for Hannah's wonderful hymn, the prototype for Mary's Magnificat.

Elkanah, Hannah, and Peninnah

As Samson's story begins with notices of geography and paternal family, so does the story of Samuel. Most family histories are interesting only if we know the people and the places. For me, 1 Samuel 1:1 is not promising: "There was a certain man of Ramathaim, a Zuphite from the hill country of Ephraim, whose name was Elkanah son of Jeroham son of Elihu son of Tohu son of Zuph, an Ephraimite." At least we can determine that Elkanah comes from a well-known and likely respected family. While Samson is a Danite, with that tribe's various problematic connections, Elkanah is an Ephraimite from "the hill country of Ephraim." He's right at home.

Ephraim is the younger (and therefore more important) of Jacob's two sons. The "hill country of Ephraim" receives thirty-one mentions in the Bible, including the notice that Joshua, Moses's successor, was buried there (Joshua 24:30; Judges 2:9), as was Eleazar the son of Aaron the high priest, Moses's brother (Joshua 24:33). The judge Ehud led a successful charge from there (Judges 3:27), and the "hill country of Ephraim" is where Deborah the judge sat under her palm tree to resolve disputes among the Israelites (Judges 4:5). Gideon sent messengers throughout the hill country of Ephraim (Judges 7:24). However, this location is also where apostasy occurred. Judges 19, the story of the Levite's concubine, a story that epitomizes the decline of the Israelites, begins in the "hill country of Ephraim." In later history, it is the site of Shechem, later Samaria, the capital of the Northern Kingdom of Israel. According to Jeremiah 31:6

(the "new covenant" chapter), "There shall be a day when sentinels will call / in the hill country of Ephraim: / 'Come, let us go up to Zion, / to the LORD our God.'" When Jesus journeys to Samaria (see John 4), a story with another type scene, this one of a woman and man meeting at a well and talking about marriage, we can include 1 Samuel 1 in the background.

The genealogy also tells us that Elkanah is not a priest, for he is not a Levite. Nor is he from the tribe of Judah, so that we know he will not be the father of David. Jacob had announced, "The scepter shall not depart from Judah, / nor the ruler's staff from between his feet, / until tribute comes to him, / and the obedience of the peoples is his" (Genesis 49:10); Saul, who is a Benjaminite, is doomed before he is anointed. More interesting, the phrase in Genesis 49:10 that the NRSVue translates "until tribute comes" is, in Hebrew, "until Shiloh comes." Shiloh is at the time the Israelites' major worship site. It was at Shiloh that the ark of the covenant, brought by the Israelites through the wilderness, was located (see 1 Samuel 4:3). Judges 21:19 not only mentions a yearly festival there, but also gives the GPS: "north of Bethel, on the east of the highway that goes up from Bethel to Shechem and south of Lebonah." The thick geographical detail gives a "you are there" sense. Anyone could go.

But the word can also mean "what is due to him" and so, "tribute." Both Jews and Christians in reception history have connected this verse not only to David, but also to the Messiah (for Christians, Jesus; for Jews, a future son of David).

The plot begins in the next verse, which shifts focus from Elkanah to his wives: genealogy and location may be his, but the story, like that of Sarah and Hagar and Mrs. Manoah, substantially belongs to the wives: "He had two wives; the name of one was Hannah, and the name of the other Peninnah. Peninnah had children, but Hannah had no children" (1 Samuel 1:2). The name Hannah comes from the Hebrew *chanan* (the *ch* is a guttural, as in Bach), meaning "favor" or "grace." Its English derivatives also include Ann, Anne, Anna, and Chana. In the Bible, it frequently shows up in prayers that begin, "If I have found *favor* in your eyes…" ((NIV; see, e.g., Genesis 18:3, where Abraham greets the visitors: "If I find favor with you, do not pass by your servant"). The term also appears in the famous high priestly blessing, "The LORD make his face to shine upon you and be *gracious* to you" (Numbers 6:2525, emphasis added).

The name Peninnah means "jewel" or perhaps "pearl." We have a choice: would we rather be known as "full of grace," or "highly favored," which is one translation of Luke 1:28, the angel's greeting to Mary (see also John 1:14 in relation to Jesus; Acts 6:8 in relation to Stephen), or do we want to be known as a jewel: impressive, expensive, beautifully constructed? Continuing with etymology, the *el* in Elkanah is the generic term for "god," and *kanah* means to acquire or redeem (it's the root of the name Cain). Elkanah means "acquired by God" or "redeemed by God." Ironically, it also describes the fate of his son Samuel, who will be acquired by God.

Mention of Hannah and Peninnah strikes echoes of Hagar and Sarah, Leah and Rachel. We know from the convention that there will be rivalry, although we can also anticipate détente.

When the angel sends the pregnant Hagar back to Abraham and Sarah, there is no further word of abuse. Rachel and Leah do work together. Finally, we can anticipate that Hannah who, like Mrs. Manoah, "had no children," will have children. An angel may arrive, or maybe not.

This family is faithful. We know little about the religiosity of Manoah and his wife, but that the angel warns against unclean things may indicate non-kosher food in the house. Conversely, with Elkanah, "This man used to go up year by year from his town to worship and to sacrifice to the LORD of hosts at Shiloh, where the two sons of Eli, Hophni and Phinehas, were priests of the LORD" (1 Samuel 1:3). Elkanah and his wives represent faithful families, and so anticipate Elizabeth and Zechariah, Mary and Joseph. They are not going to see and be seen; they are going to worship. No holiday is mentioned, so the family could be participating in their own annual sacrifice.

Such shrines as Shiloh were common in Israel until the late seventh century BCE when King Josiah limited sacrifice to the Temple on Mount Zion in Jerusalem (the move was great for Jerusalem's economy, but it put Levites in places like the hill country in Ephraim out of business).

While Eli is the priest, his sons are the local functionaries. The name Eli means "My God," a good Hebrew name. The sons have Egyptian names, as does Moses. Hophni may mean "tadpole"; "Phinehas," the same name as one of Aaron's zealous grandson (Exodus 6:25; Numbers 25, and elsewhere) means "Nubian" or "bronze skin." The names connect the family to Egypt, as does an oracle in 1 Samuel 2:27: "A man of God came to Eli and said to him, 'Thus the LORD has said: I revealed myself to the family of your ancestor in Egypt when they were slaves to the house of Pharaoh.'" We have here another text-critical problem. The reference in 1 Samuel 2:27 to "slaves" appears in the Greek and in Qumran manuscripts, but not in the Hebrew (Masoretic) texts. From the Hebrew, one could conclude that the family had Egyptian origins.

Connections to Moses continue. At the end of Samson's story, we find the Danites employing Moses's son in false worship, and in 1 Samuel 2:29 we read that Eli's sons were "fattening [them]selves on the choicest parts of every offering" (1 Samuel 2:29), that is, skimming off the top. Competent and honorable leaders do not always produce children in their image and likeness. Therefore, the prophet explains to Eli that while God "promised that your family and the family of your ancestor should go in and out before me forever, but now the LORD declares: Far be it from me, for those who honor me I will honor, and those who despise me shall be treated with contempt" (1 Samuel 2:30). The Philistines (still here from Samson's time) will capture the ark, Hophni and Phinehas die that day, and then Eli dies.

Elkanah's family have problems of a different sort. Elkanah would offer sacrifice, and as is the case with all sacrifices except "whole burnt offerings," he gave some of the meat to the priests and shared the rest with his family. Going to a sanctuary and, later, to the Jerusalem Temple—the first, built by David's son Solomon, is decades away from construction—was a rare (or well done) occasion for worshippers to eat meat. Elkanah gave "portions to his wife Peninnah and to all her sons and daughters, but to Hannah he gave a double [something— probably "portion"— the Hebrew is not clear] because he loved her, though the LORD had closed her womb" (1 Samuel 1:4-5). This explicit love reveals, in retrospect, that we are never told that Abraham loved Sarah. Usually the Bible does not tell us how couples feel about each other. When it does, I take the occasion as a reminder to tell the people I love that I love them.

I also appreciate the attention both the narrator and Elkanah give to Hannah. Her inability to conceive is not regarded as the result of sin. Recognizing infertility to be a disability then allows us to see the double portion as a type of compensation. There is nothing Elkanah can do to make her feel better, but he tries. I also wonder, and I may be stretching, if Hannah is, despite her husband's care, undernourished or even anorexic (which may account for her infertility). Has her desperation for a child created a psychological sense that her body has betrayed her? At the end of the story, we learn that Hannah, finally, both eats and drinks, and it is then that she conceives.

The trip to Shiloh continues, year after year. Continuing also is Peninnah's provocation. Now Hannah is in Sarah's position, provoked by a co-wife who looked at her as a lightweight. Peninnah's provocation need not be verbal; it may be that her mere existence was a provocation to Hannah. No wonder "Hannah wept and would not eat" (1 Samuel 1:7); she lives in a family filled with children who are not hers.

Elkanah notices her pain. Calling her by name, he asks, "Hannah, why do you weep? Why do you not eat? Why is your heart sad? Am I not more to you than ten sons?" (1 Samuel 1:8). Poor man; he doesn't, he cannot, understand. No, dear Elkanah, you are not more than ten sons. Loving spouses can fulfill some of the partner's needs, but not all, whether that need is for a child or a career or a separate identity. Elkanah does not feel the pain Hannah feels each time Peninnah starts showing, gives birth, nurses, remarks on a new tooth or a first step. He has children; she does not. It is not his body that yearns to be pregnant; hers does.

I am reminded of Ruth 4:15, where after Ruth gives birth to a son, the women of Bethlehem tell her mother-in-law Naomi, "He shall be to you a restorer of life and a nourisher of your old age, for your daughter-in-law who loves you, who is more to you than seven sons, has borne him." Naomi's son Mahlon had been married to Ruth, but he and his brother are both dead. The grandchild, whatever comfort he provides, is still not more than Naomi's two dead children.

Despite Elkanah's attempt to understand his wife, the text does not mention that he prays for her to conceive. Then again, this is a story about silent prayer. Perhaps in offering sacrifice, his prayer for Hannah also ascended. Absence of evidence is not evidence of absence.

Nor does Hannah say to him, as did Rachel to Jacob, "Give me children, or I shall die" (Genesis 30:1). Hannah says nothing to him, just as she says nothing to Peninnah. There is nothing to say.

The Bible gives voice to those who, like Hannah, yearn for a child. At the same time the Bible does not say that all women want children, or that all women feel shame or loss without them. Here the story of Manoah and his wife is helpful, as is the story of the Great Woman of Shunem, who showed hospitality to the prophet Elisha. They did not ask for a child, or pray for one, and they were probably doing just fine without them. Miriam, the sister of Moses and Aaron, has no children. Neither does Deborah the judge. Neither do most of the women we meet in the Gospels (Mary Magdalene, Mary and Martha, Joanna, Anna in the Temple, and others). Not all women, or all men, have the same needs.

The Vow

Leaving Elkanah's question about his worth unanswered, Hannah remains distressed. She neither eats nor drinks nor responds to questions. The rest of the family, meanwhile, continues with business as usual. They are at the sanctuary; it's time to eat and drink. As for Hannah, her throat was constricted with grief. No words come out; no food goes in.

Following the meal, Hannah gets up. Now she, like Hagar, starts to show agency. Rather than have a heart-to-heart with Elkanah, she "presented herself before the LORD" (1 Samuel 1:9a). She will present her son Samuel to Eli. People present gifts on the altar; people do not generally present themselves to God. To present oneself to the divine is to be fully present. It is both to have the courage to state the truth and the vulnerability of needing an answer. She speaks words to God that she will not speak to her husband or to her co-wife.

Hannah is the first woman to make such a presentation. The visitors came to Abraham; the angel visits Hagar at the well and Mrs. Manoah at the field. They are recipients of revelation, not initiators. Hannah acts. She goes to the sanctuary, alone, to tell God what she needs.

From Hannah's desperation, the narrative turns to Eli the priest, "sitting on the seat beside the doorpost of the temple of the Lord" (1 Samuel 1:9b). His sons are doing the work of the shrine; Eli sits. I am reminded of Mrs. Manoah, sitting in the field, or Abraham, sitting at the door of his tent. All three will receive revelation. Perhaps sitting—not being occupied with other matters—is a good time to be open to a divine presence, or a person in need. Alternatively, the text says nothing about Eli's wife or about any grandchildren. He seems alone, perhaps feeling no longer useful. No one seeks his advice; no divine presence envelops him. He sits.

We can add a sidenote on Eli's grandchildren. When Phineas's wife was pregnant, she heard the news that the Philistines had captured the ark and that her husband and father-in-law had died. Dying in childbirth, she names her son Ichabod, which means "'the glory has departed from Israel,' because the ark of God had been captured and because of her father-in-law and her husband" (1Samuel 4:21). Not all children will be raised by their biological mothers.

While Eli sits, we return to Hannah, who was "deeply distressed and prayed to the Lord and wept bitterly" (1 Samuel 1:10). The verbs predicated of Hannah contrast with Eli's inaction. I would have expected Eli, had he any pastoral sense, to offer comfort: a cup of water, a kind smile. But, nothing. He sits.

Hannah now speaks, "O LORD of hosts, if only you will look on the misery of your servant and remember me and not forget your servant" (1 Samuel 1:11a). There is so much to say about this phrase.

First, Hannah demonstrates the value of lament. Distressed and weeping bitterly, she does not hide her misery. She both shows God how she feels and tells God how she feels. I can hear her say, "My God, my God, why have you forsaken me? / Why are you so far from helping me, from the words of my groaning? / O my God, I cry by day, but you do not answer; / and by night but find no rest" (Psalm 22:1-2). She imagines herself mocked by Peninnah's presence, and each time she sees a mother with a child she thinks, "All who see me mock me; / they sneer at me; they shake their heads" (Psalm 22:7). Psalm 22:9-10—"Yet it was you who took me from the womb; / you kept me safe on my mother's breast. / On you I was cast from my birth, / and since my mother bore me you have been my God"—is both pathetic in relation to Hannah's needs and predictive in relation to the dedication of Samuel to God. Any prayer in the Bible—a psalm, Hannah's prayers in 1 Samuel 1 and 2, Mary's Magnificat—can be prayed by anyone.

Second, Hannah's first words are "O LORD of hosts." The epithet suggests a heavenly court, which allows the contrast: God has myriads of attendants, could Hannah not have just one child? Rabbi Elazar, quoted in the *Babylonian Talmud, Berakot* 31a-b, suggests that Hannah was making an analogy: God is the master of all of creation, hosts upon hosts; could he therefore not grant her one son? Then the rabbi offers a parable, with the formula "to what is this similar...": A king makes a feast for his servants. A poor person, standing at the door, begs for one piece of bread, but the people at the feast ignore him. Finally, pushing his way into the room he stands before the king, and he notes that with the great feast, surely a piece of bread can be spared. Jesus, the storyteller himself, would have liked this one.

Third, just as Hagar named *El-roi*, the God who sees, so Hannah is the first person in the Bible to call God the "Lord of hosts" (Hebrew: *YHWH tzeva'ot*). When we address God, we find the title that works best for us: father, shepherd, rock, source, Lord.

Fourth, Hannah cries, "Remember me!" This is the same cry Samson voiced when, blinded and bound in the Philistine temple, he "called to the Lord and said, 'Lord God, remember me and strengthen me only this once, O God, so that with this one act of revenge I may pay back the Philistines for my two eyes'" (Judges 16:28). Hannah asks for new life; Samson asks for a good death. The call to God to "remember," which appears frequently in Israel's Scriptures, prompts us to ask both "For what do we want to be remembered?" and "For what do we need to be reminded?"

The theme of divine memory is like a drumbeat, or a heartbeat, throughout the Scriptures of Israel. It resounds when, following the Flood, God states, "I will remember my covenant that is between me and you and every living creature of all flesh, and the waters shall never again become a flood to destroy all flesh" (Genesis 9:15). Memory is like a heavenly life preserver; as long as we are remembered, we still live.

In Exodus 32:13, Moses prays to God, "Remember Abraham, Isaac, and Israel, your servants, how you swore to them by your own self, saying to them, 'I will multiply your descendants like the stars of heaven, and all this land that I have promised I will give to your descendants, and they shall inherit it forever.'" There are another two hundred or so appeals, whether asking God to remember the covenants, or asking the people to remember those same covenants, or their experience in Egypt.

Fifth is Hannah's self-reference, "your servant . . . your servant." The Hebrew (and Greek) can also be translated "your slave . . . your slave." The KJV gives "handmaid," which prior to Margaret Atwood's novel and the television show based on it was quaint, and after is unthinkable. The self-definition connects Hannah to Mary, the "slave of the Lord" (Luke 1:38; NRSVue "servant") as well as to other "slaves" [NRSVue "servants"] of the Lord: Moses (Deuteronomy 34:5 and many other places), Joshua (Joshua 24:29), David (Psalm 18:0), Isaiah's suffering figure (Isaiah 42:19). If we take this title for ourselves, how do we understand its connotations?

Sixth, Hannah's prayer is personal: Remember *me*. Not every prayer needs to be for world peace. Prayers can be, indeed should be, also personal.

Seventh, she specifies: she wants a "male child" or, as both the Hebrew and Greek literally read, "seed of men." The expression can connote a "great" or "important" man, someone who will stand out. Alternatively, it could mean one man among many, an average fellow. We can speculate as to what she wants, and so what we wish for our children or grandchildren, or for ourselves. Do we want importance in the public eye: a commemorative coin; a ticker-tape parade; access to the proverbial halls of power? These are more or less what Hannah's son Samuel will have. Or, do we want for them, or for us, a happy and fulfilled life? Or both?

Finally, Hannah vows, "Then I will set him before you as a nazirite until the day of his death. He shall drink neither wine nor intoxicants, and no razor shall touch his head" (1 Samuel 1:11b). Connections to Samson, as well as to John the Baptizer, abound.

Hannah's prayer is a type of bargaining. Let me get an A on this paper; let me get into this graduate program; let me get this job; let me win the lottery, and I'll tithe, quit smoking, stop drinking, work in a soup kitchen. Usually the "then I'll do X" is what we ought to be doing in the first place. Bargaining with God can make prayer transactional.

The judge Jephthah made such a bargain, and it resulted in the death of his daughter. This comparison to Jephthah makes me wonder: Elkanah is not present when Hannah makes her vow, so what did he think? The child she promises to dedicate to God is also his child. Should the father have a say in its implementation?

Hannah is not the only one who makes obedience transactional. The patriarch Jacob, at Beth-el (the name means "House of God"), "made a vow, saying, 'If God will be with me and will keep me in this way that I go and will give me bread to eat and clothing to wear, so that I come again to my father's house in peace, then the Lord shall be my God and this stone, which I have set up for a pillar, shall be God's house, and of all that you give me I will surely give one-tenth to you'" (Genesis 28:20-22). Then again, Jacob has nothing to lose. Were he to die, he could not continue to worship God.

It may be helpful to think about why we, or some of us, make such prayers. Perhaps we are thinking of God as on automatic: If I do this, then God will do that. We know better, but that knowledge does not stop us from such bargains. Better, such prayers allow us to show a form of gratitude; they give us a form of agency. As for vows that can harm, such as the one Jephthah makes, or vowing resources to a religious institution and so potentially depriving family members of their needs (see Mark 7 and Matthew 15), rabbinic Judaism teaches that any vow leading to harm not only can be, but should be, revoked (*Babylonian Talmud, Sanhedrin* 68a).

Despite Hannah's heartfelt prayer and weeping, Eli "observed her mouth. Hannah was praying silently; only her lips moved, but her voice was not heard; therefore, Eli thought she was drunk" (1 Samuel 1:12-13). While silent prayer, like silent reading, was likely a rarity, his lack of sympathy strikes me as harsh. Perhaps he is thinking of his own debauched sons. Perhaps he cannot see the good in anyone, given his familial situation, as Hannah could not see the good in her own life, given her familial situation.

Or perhaps Eli expected different, more composed behavior at the sanctuary. Decades ago when people in churches started to raise their hands when reciting the "Our Father," it seemed to me odd or even show-off-y. I judged the unfamiliar negatively

(I should have known better). Many of us expect the "polite" form of prayer, where emotions are not on display. Decorum may keep the service humming along nicely, but it can get in the way of authentic religious experience. What is decorous to one person may seem inauthentic or, well, barren, to another.

Not only does Eli think Hannah is drunk, he attempts to humiliate her by asking, "How long will you make a drunken spectacle of yourself? Put away your wine" (1 Samuel 1:14). In calling Hannah out, Eli seeks to make a spectacle of her. The kinder move with anyone who is drunk is not to humiliate; it is to care. Nor was Hannah drunk. Facing such emotional displays, people often do not know what to do. They hush; they shush; they look away. This is the time for kindness, not judgment.

Hannah now maintains her composure. She does not say, "Butt out" or "You idiot." Her eloquent response makes clear that she is not drunk, not out of control, not—to use the term commonly applied to women in such situations—hysterical. "No, my lord" she starts. She addresses him respectfully. Perhaps she knows him. She and the family had been going to Shiloh year after year; perhaps she knows that he is broken and in despair himself. Perhaps she can find empathy where he could not.

She explains, "I am a woman deeply troubled; I have drunk neither wine nor strong drink, but I have been pouring out my soul before the Lord. Do not regard your servant as a worthless woman, for I have been speaking out of my great anxiety and vexation all this time" (1 Samuel 1:15-16). It takes courage to admit that one is anxious and vexed. Further, Hannah had vowed that were she to have a son, she would make him a perpetual nazirite. Here she affirms her maternal role: Like Mrs. Manoah, she has avoided wine and strong drink. Her prayer is both passionate and sober.

Jewish tradition makes Hannah's prayer the model for how to pray. The *Babylonian Talmud, Berakot* 31a-b concludes from the fact that Hannah's lips moved in her silent prayer, that in prayer, we should move our lips. This approach prevents us from rushing through or speed reading; it brings the body into prayer; it means, ideally, that we think about what we are saying rather than going on automatic. Next, it notes that some prayers should be said silently even when we are praying in communal contexts. There are times we raise our voices together, and there are times when we pray as individuals. Finally, the tradition approves Hannah's reproach to Eli: One who is suspected of doing something wrong must correct the impression. Further, it insists that the one who held the incorrect view, upon being corrected, should reconcile with a blessing, just as Eli, corrected, said to Hannah, "Go in peace" (1 Samuel 1:17a).

Although Eli doesn't apologize for misjudging Hannah (were I writing this text, I would have included an apology), he more or less admits his mistake.

Now comes the annunciation, taking the form of a blessing. Eli prays, "The God of Israel grant the petition you have made to him" (1 Samuel 1:17b). Hannah assents, "Let your servant find favor in your sight" (1 Samuel 1:18a). Beneath the term "find favor" is the Hebrew *chen*, the root of the name Hannah.

Beneath "servant" is *shifchah*, the same term used for Hagar in Genesis 16. I wonder if Hannah were engaging in a double entendre. Did she think of herself as Eli's servant, or was she rather continuing to pray, for she sees herself as God's servant, and it is in God's sight that she prays to be remembered.

Hannah then acts as if her prayer has already been answered. We see her as she "went her way and ate and drank" (the Septuagint, and so the NRSVue, adds "with her husband," perhaps to clarify that there was no hanky-panky with the priest or that she did not stop off at the pub). The Septuagint also adds, "her countenance was sad no longer." The Hebrew, which is difficult to translate, may be a pun. It reads literally something like "and before her face not was there to her still." The term beneath "her face" sounds very much like "Peninnah," as if perhaps Peninnah is no longer a vexation. The rivalry is over. Hannah is not yet pregnant, but she is assured that she will become so. She does not laugh like Sarah, flee like Hagar, or have a chat with her husband, as did Mrs. Manoah. Multiple reactions are appropriate.

The Fulfillment

The family rises early the next morning, worships God, and returns home. "Elkanah knew his wife Hannah, and the LORD remembered her." Her prayer has been answered. It is answered not by an arrangement with a co-wife, not by a miracle given the ages of the parties, not by what may be an angelic conception. It is answered by a man who loves his wife but who realizes that he cannot be everything for her. It is answered by

Hannah herself, who risks yet another failure to conceive. And it is answered by God.

This part of the story ends by noting that "In due time Hannah conceived and bore a son. She named him Samuel, for she said, 'I have asked him of the LORD'" or, better, "I asked YHWH for him" (1 Samuel 1:20). The problem here is that the Hebrew term for "to ask" is *sha'al*, and it is a better origin for the name "Saul" than it is for "Samuel." On the other hand, the story does contain a great deal of asking: about emotions, actions; for children. The name Samuel likely derives from the Hebrew *shem*, meaning "name," and *el* is, as noted above for Elkanah, the generic term for "god." *Shmoo-el*, which is how the name is pronounced in Hebrew, thus means something like "His name is El." The one who bears the name carries the voice of God. It's quite a responsibility to place on a child.

Hannah keeps her son with her until he is weaned: she will fulfill her vow, "that he may appear in the presence of the LORD and remain there forever" (1 Samuel 1:22) but not just yet (I am reminded of St. Augustine's "Give me chastity and continence, but not yet"). Elkanah leaves the decision to her. Numbers 30:8, part of a longer section on vows, discusses the possibility that a husband can overrule his wife's vow: "But if, at the time that her husband hears of it, he overrules her, then he shall nullify the vow by which she was obligated or the thoughtless utterance of her lips by which she bound herself, and the LORD will forgive her." A widow or divorced woman is free to make whatever vow she wants, but a wife is constrained, since her vow may well impact the husband.

Elkanah's comment, "Do what seems best to you" (1 Samuel 1:23; literally, "do the good in your eyes"), has implications for his own life. His words echo what Abraham says when Sarah complains about Hagar: "Do to her as you please" (Genesis 16:6; literally "do to her the good in your eyes"). In both cases, the men risk losing their children. Hagar, pregnant, returns to Abraham and Sarah's home, but Sarah will again cause her to leave. Hannah will give her son to Eli at the sanctuary of Shiloh, where Eli will function as a surrogate father.

While Elkanah, Peninnah, and the other children make their annual pilgrimage to Shiloh, Hannah stays home. One wonders what Eli was thinking when he saw them. What convesations might they have had? Did Eli offer pastoral care to the rest of the family, or did he just sit?

After three years, Hannah brings the child, along with impressive sacrificial offerings (Elkanah and his family are well off) to Shiloh and presents him to Eli. The scene ends with everyone worshipping God.

Each year when the family went to Shiloh, Hannah would bring him "a little robe" (1 Samuel 2:19). I picture her knitting, as I did for my children, as my mother did for me, and as my mother-in-law, who died the week I was drafting this chapter, did for her sons and grandchildren.

A Few Thoughts

Our story opens in a completely male world: Elkanah's home; Elkanah's ancestry; Elkanah's wives and their status in terms of how many children they gave him; Elkanah's going up to the shrine; Elkanah's offering the sacrifice; Elkanah's distributing the portions. At the end, we do not (or at least most of us do not) remember Elihu son of Tohu son of Zuph or even the name of Hannah's husband. The story thus shifts our sense of what is important, and when.

According to 1 Samuel 2:20, when Hannah would visit with Samuel and Elkanah would come to offer sacrifice, "Eli would bless Elkanah and his wife and say, 'May the LORD repay you with children by this woman for the loan that she made to the LORD.'" Eli could have mentioned Hannah by name. The prayerbook (Hebrew *siddur*, meaning "order," and from the same root as *seder*, the Passover meal) we used in the synagogue when I was a child had a line something like, "Bless the members of this congregation, their wives and their children." I bristled at this. My father died when I was young, so my mother was the full "member of the congregation."

I also wonder about Peninnah and her children. Has she died? Are the children now with families of their own and going to Shiloh? More, did she think of herself as another Leah, fertile but unloved? Was she exhausted from caring for her children, while Hannah embroidered or baked or gardened...or moisturized or put her hair in an updo...or spent her time lamenting, or moping? At the end of Hannah's story, Peninnah's absence is, ironically, more present. In a story about memory and taking note, whom do we forget?

The last mention of Hannah is in 1 Samuel 2:21: "And the LORD took note of Hannah; she conceived and bore three sons and two daughters. And the boy Samuel grew up in the presence of the LORD." I do not want to think of these other, nameless, three sons and two daughters as compensation prizes. Nor do I think that Hannah will somehow miss Samuel less because she has other children. Each one is special. Each one is to be loved. They, too, will have stories to tell.

Hannah will be remembered in the prophet Anna, who greets the baby Jesus in the Temple (see Luke 2:36-37). She will be remembered in the postbiblical story of the conception and birth of Mary, for Mary's mother is also named Anna. She will be remembered in Mary's Magnificat, which is modeled on her song of exaltation, liberation, and redemption. And she will be remembered every year in the synagogue, when we read 1 Samuel 1:1–2:10 on Rosh Ha-Shanah, the new year. Finally, a personal note, my mother's name was Anna (which she changed to Anne), another iteration of Hannah. As many of us realize when we get older, mothers, and fathers as well, can be much more complicated, and much more interesting, than we first thought.

CHAPTER 4

Jesus:
Heir to Traditions

In outlining and then writing the introduction and the first three chapters of this book, I kept finding connections to Jesus. Some are already well-known, and I did not want this volume to repeat my Nativity study, *Light of the World*. Readers of the Bible should be more or less familiar with how Matthew models the Nativity scenes on the life of Moses: endangered baby, flight to Egypt, return from Egypt, crossing water (the Baptism), temptation in the wilderness, then ascending a mountain, as Moses went up Mount Sinai, to teach Torah to his followers. Well-known also is how Matthew quotes Isaiah 7:14, in the Greek, to show that the virginal conception of Jesus to Mary fulfills prophecy. In reading Matthew 1–2 and Luke 1–2 in the light of, or with attentions to the echoes sounding from the earlier texts, we see much more.

This vision, or hearing, goes in multiple directions. On the one hand, the comparison helps us notice overlooked parts of the Gospels. On the other, when we read the older stories after reading the Gospels, we can find new things there too. This back-and-forth model is substantially how memory works. As we retell the stories of our past—whether personal or familial or community-based, we adapt those stories based on our own new experiences and on the needs of our audiences. Memory also takes discrete moments and then organizes them, as if putting beads of different sizes and colors on a string, determining what to foreground, what to juxtapose, and what to ignore.

The authors we call Matthew and Luke (the original texts are anonymous) had in their memories the stories of the births of Ishmael and Isaac, Moses, Samson, and Samuel. They expected some who would read their Gospels to know those stories, draw connections, and encourage members in their assemblies to become better familiar wth the Septuagint, the "Scriptures" these Greek-speakers had. Matthew and Luke did not know the word "Christmas," and they would not have thought of Santa Claus and elves, tinsel and stockings, carols and trees and candy canes, the Grinch and Burgermeister Meisterburger. If we move away from these later stories and tradition and move backward to the ancient Hebrew texts, we find that good stories beget good stories, that there is delight in plays on conventions, that the stories prompt us to ask questions not only about the narratives they present but also about our own lives and values. We find that the stories in the Old Testament helped birth the stories in the Gospels.

As I read and reread the stories in Genesis, Judges, and 1 Samuel, here are several of the vignettes that surfaced.

Attention to Joseph

Birth stories tend, appropriately, to feature mothers, and the husbands recede into the background. Abraham impregnates

Hagar but refuses to stop Sarah's abuse and then acquiesces to Sarah's demand that mother and child be expelled. We have no record of his speaking to Hagar either before the pregnancy or after. She must have told him what to name their child, but the Bible does not record the conversation. Concerning Isaac's birth, Sarah has the last word. Mr. Manoah is not the swiftest Danite in the Late Bronze Age, and Elkanah, supportive as he is, becomes overshadowed by Hannah and then replaced as a father both by Eli the priest and by God.

Yet we can recover the stories of fathers. When Sarah orders Abraham to send Hagar and Ishmael away, the Bible tells us, "The matter was very distressing to Abraham on account of his son" (Genesis 21:11). I imagine that Elkanah was very distressed when he learned that Hannah had vowed to give their son to God by entrusting him to Eli at Shiloh. Both Abraham and Elkanah had other children, but one does not substitute for another. Manoah appears to feel left out already at the annunciation, as if he could not be part of his son's life. The Bible notices, and affirms, not only maternal but also paternal love, paternal emotion, and paternal loss. Real men in the Bible have—and show—feelings. The Stoics gave us Stoicism; ancient Israel gives us honest emotions.

Attention to these men brings me to Joseph.

While Joseph is prominently featured in Matthew's Nativity account, he is never named in Mark's Gospel. John mentions him twice as "Jesus son of Joseph" (John 1:45; 6:42), but the extensive references to God as "father" in John fully overshadow Joseph. In introducing Joseph, Luke neatly tucks him between references to Mary: "In the sixth month [that is, the sixth month of Elizabeth's pregnancy], the angel Gabriel was sent by God to a town in Galilee called Nazareth, to a virgin engaged to a man whose name was Joseph, of the house of David. The virgin's name was Mary" (Luke 1:26-27). For Luke, Joseph's role is to provide Mary a fiancé and to provide Jesus a connection to King David. He receives no angelic annunciation or revelatory dream.

After Mary receives the annunciation, she doesn't go to Joseph. Instead, she leaves town to visit her cousin Elizabeth, and she stays with Elizabeth for three months (Luke 1:56), that is, until Elizabeth is in her ninth month and is ready to give birth. Three months, and there is no word about Joseph.

The next time Luke mentions Joseph is in the next chapter, where, following the notice of the Roman census, we read, "Joseph also went from the town of Nazareth in Galilee to Judea, to the city of David called Bethlehem, because he was descended from the house and family of David" (Luke 2:4). Now it is Joseph's turn to travel, but while Mary had gone alone to Judea, Joseph takes Mary with him. I'd like to think that he did not want to leave her alone and that he wanted to be with Mary when she gave birth. I'd like to think that Mary wanted Joseph to be there as well.

Joseph's connection to Bethlehem provides the rationale for Mary, who lives in Nazareth, to give birth to the "son of David" in the "city of David," since "[Joseph] went to be registered with Mary, to whom he was engaged and who was expecting a child" (Luke 2:5). But he is more than his lineage, as are Abraham, Amram (Moses's father), Manoah, and Elkanah.

Then nothing about Joseph until the shepherds find "Mary and Joseph and the child lying in the manger" (Luke 2:16). Joseph has been present throughout; to find Mary and the child is to find him. That Luke again tucks him in grammatically between Mary and the child reminds me of that earlier verse, "In the sixth month . . . Mary." Now he can be seen as the center point who cares for both. He is important here for his presence, not just for his lineage.

Finally, Luke mentions that the family went to Jerusalem for pilgrimage festivals (2:41)—as Elkanah and his family went to Shiloh to offer sacrifices and to pray. One year they started the return home without noticing that the boy Jesus had remained behind. Jesus at this time is twelve years old, old enough for a sense of personal responsibility. I doubt Luke's story is simply an earlier version of the *Home Alone* movies with the less-than-adept parents. They expected Jesus to be responsible, and in ways they could not yet understand he was. Finding Jesus in the Jerusalem Temple (an enormous edifice), Mary asks, "Child, why have you treated us like this? Your father and I have been anxiously looking for you" (Luke 2:48).

By "your father," she means Joseph. She names Joseph "father." She values him. Mary explains that not only she but also Joseph have been frantic in their seeking. Jesus replies, "Why were you searching for me? Did you not know that I must be in my Father's house?" (Luke 2:49) or "about the matters of my father" (my translation). Joseph is standing right there. The comment is heartbreaking. I shudder to imagine how Joseph reacted. Mary refers to Joseph as the boy's father, but Jesus rejects the relationship.

Luke 2:50 explains that Mary and Joseph "did not understand what he said to them." Socially, Jesus is an adolescent, and adolescents are not always articulate. Theologically, they do not understand, even with Gabriel's annunciation to Mary, what this child will do.

The next verse notes that Jesus "went down with them" [one always goes up to and down from Jerusalem] to Nazareth and "was obedient to them." Both parents came back with him; he attended to both. Luke notes that "his mother treasured all these things in her heart" (verse 51), but does not note what Joseph thought. Twelve years earlier, when Mary and Joseph together presented baby Jesus in the Temple, Simeon told Mary that "a sword will pierce your own soul" (Luke 2:35). That sword would have also pierced Joseph's soul.

The final line in this story and our last notice of Joseph, Luke 2:52, is that "Jesus increased in wisdom and in years [or stature] and in divine and human favor." In showing obedience to Mary and Joseph perhaps part of this wisdom, the wisdom of an adolescent growing up, is the recognition of what Joseph had done for him.

The *Protevangelium of James* depicts Joseph as an elderly man at the time that he and Mary wed, and Joseph promises to guard Mary's virginity. Historically, Joseph would have been about thirty and Mary about twenty, the average age Jewish men and women married at the time. If we think of him as elderly, then we can easily explain his absence in the stories of Jesus's adult life by determining that he had died.

Today we speak of the heartbreak of mothers who lose their children. We have Mothers Against Drunk Drivers; there are the Madres de Plaza de Mayo in Buenos Aires who began protesting over their "disappeared" children back in 1977. In Iran is the group known as "mourning mothers"; in China are the Tiananmen mothers; in Turkey there are the "Saturday mothers"; the organization Madre has a global outreach, the list goes on. Mary and Elizabeth—women whose sons are killed by government officials—are precursors of these groups, just as earlier in the biblical tradition are other mothers whose sons have died, starting with Eve. These mothers are joined by Mrs. Manoah, whose son Samson, captured by Philistines, dies in captivity.

Jesus's last words to Joseph are heart-breaking. But I imagine that Joseph knows his son will forge his own path and forgives him for this unintended hurt.

Stories Parents Tell Their Children

In both Matthew and Luke, one of Joseph's major roles, if not *the* major role, is to anchor Jesus into David's family. Paul is also concerned about this connection, for he begins his letter to the Romans by speaking of "the gospel concerning his Son, who was descended from David according to the flesh" (Romans 1:3).

Paternity is not the only deciding factor of identity. Indeed, sometimes it goes missing. In putting all these stories together, I suddenly realized (sometimes I'm slow) that Moses is raised by Pharaoh's daughter, but there is no indication that someone plays the "father" role in the Egyptian palace. Nor does his biological father, Amram, play a role in the Bible other than the notice that he was the father of Aaron, Miriam, and Moses. Samson's ostensive father, Manoah, will attempt to control his son, and he will fail. Samuel is raised by the priest Eli, himself the failed father of Hophni and Phinehas, his two sons who abuse their priestly privileges.

In comparison to all these other father-figures, both Elkanah and Joseph come out on top. Elkanah takes care of Hannah, the best he can, and he, like Joseph, will lose his child to divine service. He, like Joseph (in Luke's account), lacks an annunciation scene; he is absent when Hannah prays and then speaks with Eli, just as Joseph is absent when Gabriel speaks to Mary.

I wonder what Joseph would have told young Jesus about King David: that he was Jesse's seventh son, not the first, and that God cares more about what one does than about the right of succession belonging to a firstborn child? That David's great-grandmother was Ruth the Moabite (see Matthew 1:5)? Joseph may have explained that Ruth worked together with Naomi to secure their future just as the midwives, Pharaoh's daughter, Moses's mother, and Moses's sister all worked together to thwart Pharaoh's plans. These stories tell us that traditional enemies, such as the Moabites and the Egyptians, could be friends, and that not all people agree with their government's policies.

Joseph might have mentioned that God promised David a perpetual kingdom. According to 2 Samuel 7:8-17, the prophet Nathan tells David that he was chosen "from following the sheep to be a prince over my people Israel," and that God promises him, "When your days are fulfilled and you lie down with your ancestors, I will raise up your offspring after you, who shall come forth from your body, and I will establish his kingdom. He shall build a house for my name, and I will establish the throne of his kingdom forever." I can easily imagine little Jesus having dreams about King David, his father's father's father... father. Was that genealogy a call to him, a sense of his own fate? (verses 8, 12-13).

What other stories did Joseph tell Jesus about *his* genealogy: Abraham, Isaac, Jacob, Perez... Boaz the husband of Ruth, Joshua the husband of Rahab (not a biblical notice, but a midrashic one), King David and King Solomon, Jehoshaphat (I bet father and son had fun, even jumped up and down, when they got to this name), Hezekiah and Josiah. When they got to Jacob the father of Joseph, I picture little Jesus, who knew his Bible stories, saying, "Didn't we already talk about Jacob, the fellow who dreamed about a stairway to heaven, and his son Joseph, who also dreamed dreams?" Joseph would explain that the names are the same, and then perhaps ask Jesus, "What does the idea that *you* are the son of Joseph the son of Jacob suggest to you? How do you understand your past, and how might that understanding prompt you to think about your future?" Each name comes with a story.

Here's a story about the genealogy that little Jesus may have heard. Matthew 1:4 mentions "Aminadab the father of Nahshon, and Nahshon the father of Salmon." Nahshon appears in Exodus 6:23, which states that Aaron (Moses's brother) married Elisheba, daughter of Amminadab (spelled differently) and sister of Nahshon. John the Baptizer's mother is named Elizabeth, the Greek version of Elisheba.

One midrash (*Numbers Rabbah* 13) notes that when Moses led the children of Israel out of Egyptian slavery and to the shore of the Red (or Reed) Sea, the people feared drowning. Only when Nahshon ben (Hebrew for "son of") Aminadab, brother of Elisheba, put his foot in the sea did the waters part. In one version of this story, Nahshon waded into the water, deeper, deeper, until it was up to his neck, and then the waters parted. Miracles do occur, but we must be willing to risk all in partnership with the divine. Jesus learned this lesson.

Being Righteous

Stories in the Old Testament/Tanakh do not withold listing the flaws of their characters. Abraham lies by omission in telling both Pharaoh and Abimelech that Sarah is his sister and not his wife. He fails Hagar and Ishmael in agreeing with Sarah to expel them. Rabbinic sources paint Amram, Moses's father, as dooming the people to extinction by insisting that the men divorce their wives and therefore conceive no more children. Elkanah, the most sympathetic of the lot, finds himself replaced by the priest Eli. And Manoah...sigh, Manoah.

In comparison, Joseph is splendid. Matthew 1:18 notes that when Mary had been engaged to Joseph, but before they "lived together" (NRSVue; the Greek literally means "came together" and likely connotes "before they engaged in marital intimacy"), Joseph discovered Mary to be pregnant. While Luke gives us lots of details concerning timing, for example, in noting that Mary would have been three-months pregnant when she returned to Nazareth from visiting Elizabeth, Matthew does not. Perhaps

Joseph discovered the pregnancy in that third month, when he and Mary celebrated their wedding and were about to do what married couples do. He knows she is pregnant, whether because she told him or because he could see what, at three months, others could not.

Matthew 1:19 states, "Her husband Joseph, being a righteous man and unwilling to expose her to public disgrace, planned to divorce her quietly." Only he and Mary know why Joseph would seek a divorce.

The reference to divorce sends me back to those earlier stories, and I see what I missed the first time. Abraham could have divorced Sarah for failing to give him children. For the same reason, Manoah could have divorced his wife, and Elkanah could have divorced Hannah. They did not. We can only speculate why, and that they loved their wives, as Elkanah clearly did, seems to me the best answer.

Hagar and Mary

While Elizabeth, the mother of John the Baptizer, fits alongside Sarah, Rebekah, Rachel, Mrs. Manoah, Hannah, and the Great Woman of Shunem, as an infertile wife, Mary does not. The comparisons help us see her rather as connected on several levels to Hagar, the first woman to experience an annunciation, the first woman to name God, the first woman to accept the divine announcement both that her son will be extraordinary and experience not only rejoicing, but also pain.

In Luke 1, the angel speaks to Mary, who is engaged but is not married to Joseph. The engagement would likely put her in her late teens. Her age, fertility, and marital status remind me of Hagar, young and fertile, and in a relationship to Abraham that is both his "wife" and also still enslaved to Sarah. She is a wife but not quite. She is pregnant not on her own suggestion, or initial volition, but because another wanted her to become so. Sarah places Hagar into Abraham's bed. Gabriel tells Mary what God has planned for her.

The term "handmaid" is absent in the NRSVue, but it appears forty or so times in the King James Version, frequently in reference to enslaved women. Its first appearance concerns Hagar, "Now Sarai Abram's wife bare him no children: and she had a handmaid, an Egyptian, whose name was Hagar" (Genesis 16:1). In several cases, these "handmaids" are placed by their female owners in the bed of the owners' husbands. Today when we think of the twelve tribes of Israel, we recall Leah and Rachel. We should also think of Bilhah, Rachel's "handmaid" who is the mother of Dan (yes, Samson's tribe) and Naphtali. We should remember Zilpah, Leah's "handmaid," who is the mother of Gad and Asher. Ruth, a Moabite migrant laborer in Bethlehem, describes herself to Boaz the landowner (and the best catch in Bethlehem), as his "handmaiden" (Ruth 2:13; 3:9). That she also will maneuver him into marrying her adds nuance to the term. In 1 Kings 1:13, Bathsheba, the wife of David, uses it as a self-description in her attempt to ensure that her son Solomon would accede to the throne. All of these women, and their children, are part of Jesus's family as well, whether in the direct line from Joseph (so Ruth and Bathsheba), or as part of the extended family.

In the KJV translation of Luke's Gospel, the term "handmaid" or "handmaiden" is Mary's self-description. Following Gabriel's annunciation, Mary responds, "Behold the handmaid of the Lord; be it unto me according to thy word" (Luke 1:38 KJV; the NRSVue gives the more prosaic "Here am I, the servant of the Lord"). The Greek is *doulē*, "slave." Terms such as "handmaid" or "servant" sound nicer than "slave." They also help remove God from being understood as a "master" in the sense of one who "owns" slaves.

Mary, of her own free will, accepts her role as the mother of Jesus. Only free people in the Bible designate themselves as "slaves of God"; the expression can be one of complete freedom, since it indicates that no human master controls them. It is also one of complete dedication, because in antiquity, enslaved people were expected to know what their masters were thinking and act according to this will. Thus, some people today find it a helpful metaphor. Others will reject this identification; knowledge of the horrors of slavery, awareness of slavery, or enslavers, in one's own genealogy make the metaphor even more problematic.

Thinking about Mary in relationship to Hagar may help in the conversation about how the term functions. Granted they are very different: Mary is a Jew and Hagar an Egyptian; Mary is free and chooses the designation of enslaved; Hagar is enslaved, but by running seeks her freedom and by expulsion gains it. And yet, when we meet them, both are comparatively young, unmarried but by contract members of another's family, women, and childless. Neither asked to be the mother of the child they carry; both, in comparison to so many other mothers, have no difficulty in conceiving. Both receive angelic annunciations that describe what their sons will accomplish.

Both Mary and Hagar exult in their pregnancy: Hagar comes to recognize her own worth when Sarah becomes "light in her eyes" (Hebrew, a pun: like she's of less worth but also physically lighter, as Hagar is getting more and more heavy through pregnancy). Mary proclaims that God "has looked with favor on the lowly state of his servant [Greek *doulē*, "slave"]. / Surely from now on all generations will call me blessed, / for the Mighty One has done great things for me, / and holy is his name" (Luke 1:48-49). Read in connection with Hannah and stretching the grammar a bit, Luke can be understood as depicting Mary as naming God as well.

Mary proclaims that God "has come to the aid of his child Israel, / in remembrance of his mercy" (Luke 1:54). Aiding a child is what Hagar does first for her son, and then what God does for Ishmael, who is threatened with death in the wilderness, and then Isaac, who is threatened with death in the land of Moriah.

Both Hagar and Mary are told what they are to name their sons. Both will suffer as their sons suffer: Hagar fears the death of Ishmael in the wilderness, and according to John's Gospel, Mary stands by the cross as her son dies. Both will survive—and thrive. Their stories do not begin with the conception of their sons, and they do not end when the sons enter into their own fates. Hagar finds a wife for Ishmael in Egypt (Genesis 21:21) and in midrashic lore returns to Abraham. Intriguing is the mention in the Bible of a group called the "Hagrites" (1 Chronicles 5; Psalm 83:6, where they are placed in connection to the Ishmaelites, Edomites, and Moabites). We can understand this group as the descendants of Hagar. Acts 1:14 locates Mary in Jerusalem among her sons' followers, and later legend, Christian midrash, will continue to develop her stories.

In the parable of the sheep and the goats in Matthew 25, Jesus states that he is present in any person who is hungry or thirsty, naked or imprisoned. We might see Hagar and Mary as present in any who are pregnant and alone, expelled from home, or otherwise in need of compassion and resources.

Hannah and Mary

In 1 Samuel 1:11, Hannah demands that God "look on the affliction [Hebrew *oni*; Greek *tapienōsis*] of thine *handmaid* [Hebrew *amah*; Greek *doulē*]...remember me and not forget thine *handmaid*, but wilt give unto thine *handmaid* a man child..." (KJV, emphasis added; the NRSVue translates "the misery of your servant"). To reinforce this identification of enslavement, Hannah says to the priest Eli, "Count not thine *handmaid* for a daughter of Belial: for out of the abundance of my complaint and grief have I spoken hitherto" (1 Samuel 1:16 KJV, emphasis added). Finally, in 1 Samuel 1:18a (KJV), Hannah begs Eli, "Let thine *handmaid* find grace in thy sight" (empasis added).

In Mary's Magnificat (Luke 1:46-55), the "handmaid" is connected with *tapeinōsis*, "affliction," "humiliation," just as it is with Hannah. Mary speaks of the *tapeinōsin tēs doulēs*, which the NRSVue translates, "for he has looked with favor on the lowly state of his servant" (1:48). Hannah and Mary use exactly the same self-description. The KJV, inconsistent with its earlier translation, offers, "low estate of his handmaiden."

Hannah and Mary speak of themselves not as servants but as enslaved. Mary does not call herself a "servant" (that would be, in Greek, *diakonos*); she self-identifies as one enslaved (Greek: *doulē*). The connections help us find the nuance in both terms. In both cases, Hannah and Mary—free women—identify themselves. Hannah is not enslaved: she is a woman married to a relatively wealthy, polygynous husband. Mary is not enslaved: she is a woman engaged to a scion of the House of David who cares for her enough to marry her and raise a child not his own.

Hannah describes herself as enslaved to God in the hopes of conceiving a child; Mary's self-identification comes when she is already pregnant. The juxtaposition helps us think about both *how* we see ourselves in relationship to God (enslaved, a servant, disciple, child, friend, lover) and *when* we use these relational terms (petitionary prayers, thanksgiving prayers, laments). Whether this is a metaphor useful today is, as we have discussed, a difficult question.

The connection of enslavement and oppression/humiliation also connect us to the Exodus generation and so to Moses. The Egyptians seek to humiliate the Israelites, not only by enslaving them but also by dehumanizing them, by deliberately increasing their pain both physical and psychological, by ordering the killing of their children at the moment of birth, in front of their eyes. When Mary continues, "[God's] mercy is for those who fear him / from generation to generation" (Luke 1:50), we are reminded of those midwives who "feared God; they did not do as the king of Egypt commanded them, but they let the boys live" (Exodus 1:17), and "because the midwives feared God, he gave them families" (Exodus 1:21). Their names, but not that of Pharaoh or the other Egyptians, continue through the generations. As Mary proclaims that God "has come to the aid of his child Israel" (Luke 1:54), again we are reminded of those who, throughout the generation, served as the divine hands to rescue rather than to kill.

The connection of Mary to Hannah was already noted in the documents of the early Church. The *Protovangelium of James*, names Mary's mother "Anna," which is the same name as Chana in Hebrew, or Hannah. As Hannah dedicates her son Samuel to the shrine at Shiloh, so Anna dedicates her daughter Mary to the Temple in Jerusalem. The story of Hannah influenced the depiction both of Mary and of her mother, just as the story of Samuel in the shrine at Shiloh, with Eli as his new foster-father, anticipates the story of Jesus in the Jerusalem Temple, going about the matters concerning his Father.

Naming by an Angel

Mrs. Manoah names Samson, and Hannah names Samuel. Connections between Mary and Hagar, as well as Sarah and Hagar, continue in terms of an angel proclaiming what their sons are to be named. The angel told Hagar that she would bear a son and, "You shall call him Ishmael, / for the LORD has given heed to your affliction" (Genesis 16:11). In the next chapter,

God assures Abraham, "your wife Sarah shall bear you a son, and you shall name him Isaac" (17:19). God then explains, "I will establish my covenant with him as an everlasting covenant for his offspring after him."

In Matthew 1:21, the angel tells Joseph that Mary "will bear a son, and you are to name him Jesus, for he will save his people from their sins." The name "Jesus" in Hebrew comes from a root that means "salvation." Similarly, in Luke 1:31, Gabriel tells Mary that she will bear a son, whom she is to name "Jesus."

When we put the namings of Isaac and Ishmael into conversation with the naming of Jesus, more insights emerge. For example, while Genesis 22, Abraham's near-sacrifice of Isaac, is often seen as the prototype of the crucifixion of Jesus, connections of Jesus to Isaac are more substantial. Not only is Jesus a direct descendant of Isaac (Matthew 1:2), Jesus also shares in the implications of Isaac's name, which comes from the Hebrew for "laughter." While the Gospels record that "Jesus wept" (John 11:35, KJV), I think he also laughed, a lot. He would have laughed with friends at meals; he would have laughed at the humor of many of his parables. And he would have laughed when Mary smiled at him, or Joseph tickled him, or the magi made funny faces at him. Births are, if everything goes right, occasions for laughter and celebration.

Jesus is also connected to the naming of Ishmael and the predictions the angel gives to Hagar. The name Ishmael contains the Hebrew *shema*, "hear" or "listen up" or "pay attention." When Jesus tells the scribe in Mark 12:29 that the greatest commandment begins, "Hear [*shema*], O Israel: the LORD our

God, the Lord is one," we hear an echo of Ishmael's name. More, the angel tells Hagar in Genesis 16:11 that "the Lord has given heed [*shema*]—better, "heard" in the sense of "paid attention to"—to your affliction."

The term for "affliction" (Hebrew *oni*), as we have seen, not only marks many of Israel's laws, which mandate care for the socially vulnerable: the poor, the widow, the orphan, and the not-native born. It also has resonances with both Mary and Jesus. The Hebrew term *oni*, "affliction," in Genesis 16:11, comes into Greek as *tapeinōsis*. Here are a few echoes. For example, Mary exults, in the NRSVue, "For [God] has looked with favor on the lowly state of his servant" (Luke 1:48). The Greek reads, "the oppression [*tapeinōsis*] of his [female] slave." *Tapeinōsis* appears again in Acts 8:33, where it describes Jesus as Isaiah's suffering servant: "In his *tapeinōsis*—his misery, his oppression—[the NRSVue reads "humiliation"] justice was denied him."

James 1:10, using the same word, describes how the wealthy will be humiliated (NRSVue "humbled") by disappearing "like a flower in the field." The connection reminds us that to be humiliated—a public act—is a form of oppression. It is designed to create shame. It is designed not to give rise to pity but to beget rejection. The Romans stripped their victims and crucified them naked in order to humiliate them.

Hagar is the first person the Bible describes as *oni*, afflicted, oppressed, humiliated. She will not be the last. Nor, however, is affliction our final state. Paul writes, "He will transform the body of our humiliation [or 'humble body'; *tapeinōseōs*] that it may be conformed to the body of his glory [or glorious body], by the power that also enables him to make all things subject to himself" (Philippians 3:21). Our bodies can be oppressed and humiliated. Some have been slapped or beaten; some have been humiliated or shamed. That will all stop.

As for Ishmael, he is the first about whom the prediction comes that "everyone's hand" will be "against him" (Genesis 16:12). He will not be the only one. The same expression of the "hand against" occurs in Matthew 26:50, at Gethsemane, when "Then they came and laid hands on Jesus and arrested him." Jesus knows what it is like to be opposed by all, betrayed by all. Ishmael will live at odds with all his kin (Genesis 16:12), as Jesus will be rejected by his hometown, Jerusalem, even, according to Mark, his followers. But in all cases, "God hears."

Ishmael, Isaac, and Jesus are not the only children named by an angel. According to Luke 1:13, the angel Gabriel tells the elderly priest Zechariah that his equally elderly wife Elizabeth will give birth to a child, who is to be named "John." The Hebrew name *Yochanan* means "God" (the *Jo* is in Hebrew *Yo*, and it is an abbreviation for *YHWH*, which is the sacred name of God). *Chanan* in Hebrew means "grace," so the name, anglicized to John, means "God is gracious." But you already knew that, because you've already met Hannah, *Chanah*, whose name means "grace."

According to 1 Chronicles 22:9, in part of David's discussion with his son Solomon about the Temple and about Solomon's reign, David explains that God revealed to him, "A son shall be born to you; he shall be a man of rest. I will give him rest from all his enemies on every side; indeed, his name shall be Solomon, and I will give peace [Hebrew *shalom*; the word has the same letters as the name Solomon] and quiet to Israel in his days." When I think about "peace and quiet" I think about the TV being turned off and the dogs sleeping rather than barking. But peace and quiet here means that there is no sound of battle, no swords, no fear, no crying in pain. Solomon, too, according to Matthew, is an ancestor of Jesus (Matthew 1:6-7; he does not appear in Luke's genealogy), and so Jesus is also an inheritor of this concern for "peace and quiet."

They Shall Name Him Emmanuel

Matthew 1:23 offers a different name via the Greek translation of Isaiah 7:14: "They shall name him Emmanuel, which means 'God is with us.'" Here the name is not mandated by the angel; it functions instead as a title, a way the Evangelist suggests the Gospel audience should think about Jesus. The notion of God as being "with us" bookends the Gospel, first in the Nativity account and again in Matthew's last verse of the Gospel, where Jesus assures his disciples, "I am with you always" (28:20).

The Gospel of Mark, in its earliest versions, ends at 16:8, with three women fleeing in fear and silence from the empty tomb. Luke's Gospel ends with the Ascension of the resurrected Jesus into heaven and the disciples heading back to Jerusalem to wait for the Holy Spirit to descend. In John 20, the Fourth Gospel's original ending, as well as John 21, the appendix to the text, Jesus remains present with his disciples, but the

Gospel stresses that Jesus will not be with them always. In John 13:33, he tells them, "Little children, I am with you only a little longer. You will look for me, and as I said to the Jews so now I say to you, 'Where I am going you cannot come.'" The Johannine Jesus will return to his Father, but he will not leave the disciples without divine presence. He tells them, "I will ask the Father, and he will give you another Advocate, to be with you forever" (John 14:16). The Greek behind "advocate" is *paraklētos*; it means one who "stands beside" or "stands next to" (*para* is the same term in parable, paramedic and paralegal; *klētos* comes from the verb *kaleō*, which means "to call" or "to invite." Other translations include "comforter" and "defense attorney." John 14:26 identifies this *paraclete* with the Holy Spirit. To summarize: only Matthew stresses the permanent presence of Jesus, and Matthew signals this teaching with the name "Emmanuel."

Mystics will sometimes talk about a "present absence" or an "absent present." Jesus is permanently here, but not in the way he was with the disciples who were at the supper at Emmaus in Luke 24, or the ones at the shore for breakfast in John 21. I remember hearing, years ago, the "footprints in the sand" story: a dreamer walks along the beach with God and reflects over her life. She asks God why God was not there when God was most needed—the times when the sand showed only one set of footprints. God replies, "Do you see those single sets of footprints? Those are the times when I carried you." We see the same present absence at the cross, when Jesus cries, "My God, my God, why have you forsaken me?" (Matthew 27:46;

Mark 15:34). Jesus is not forsaken, for God is present in the darkness at noon. The tearing of the Temple veil is a sign of God in mourning.

Names are markers that both reveal and conceal our identities. They are also mutable; names can be changed, most commonly through marriage (my last name, Levine, is the name on my birth certificate; a few of my husbands' relatives, early on, presumed I had taken my husband's name in marriage and so called me "Amy Geller"; since I had no clue who "Amy Geller" was, both I and they were initially very confused). Others have changed their names for professional reasons (Bob Dylan was Robert Allen Zimmerman; Ralph Lauren was Ralph Lifshitz, Kirk Douglas was Issur Danielovitch Demsky, Tony Curtis was Bernard Herschel Schwartz, and Hedy Lamarr started life as Hedwig Eva Maria Kiesler). Nicknames replace given names, second names replace first names, and how we introduce ourselves necessarily says something about our identity.

Naming can also burden us, or inspire us. To be called Ishmael, God hears, means that self-identification is bound up with identity. Ishmael knew that God had heard his desperate, pregnant mother fleeing abuse; Ishmael knows that God listens. And Jesus, whose name connotes salvation, heard his commission every time his parents called to him.

One more (of many) connections related to the concern for hearing: the importance of the spoken word. Most people in antiquity were illiterate, and stories were passed through the generations not on papyrus or parchment, but on the tongue. The focus on hearing, and on the word, opens with Genesis, where God speaks the universe into being: "And God said, 'Be light'" (Genesis 1:3, my translation). The call to fidelity in Deuteronomy is not "See, Israel" or "Read, Israel" but "Hear Israel, Listen Israel." Ishmael's name means "God hears." In Luke 1:45, Mary's cousin Elizabeth exclaims, "Blessed is she who believed that there would be a fulfillment of what was spoken to her from the Lord." Even Paul, whose letters would have been read aloud to the Gentile congregations in Corinth and Philippi, Thessalonica and Galatia, wrote to the Romans, "faith comes from what is heard, and what is heard comes through the word of Christ" (Romans 10:17).

We can do even more! Early Christian theologians, wondering how conception by the Holy Spirit worked (the biology is above my pay grade), suggested that Mary conceived through her ear, when she heard the angel's word. The technical term for this is *conception per aurem*. The idea may be based on Psalm 45:10, "Hear [same Hebrew root as *shema*], O daughter, consider and incline your ear," which strikes me as a stretch, but it is consistent with the allegorical readings favored in the pre-Reformation era.

Here I Am

Connections of Jesus to Isaac and to Moses are well documented. But we can also connect Mary to Abraham, Moses, and Samuel, among others. Our concern here is the response when God calls. Immediately following the expulsion of Hagar and Ishmael, we read that "God tested Abraham" (Genesis 22:1). This is the beginning of the *Akedah* (Hebrew "binding"), the story of how Abraham bound his son Isaac on the altar and prepared to sacrifice him. Abraham is not the only figure tested by God. The term for test, in Greek, is the same word used for the "temptations" by Jesus of Satan; it appears in the "Our Father" prayer, which implores, "Lead us not into temptation" or "do not bring us to the test." The prayer adverts back to Abraham in the sense of asking God not to put us in positions where we would choose self-interest over divine service.

To begin this test—whether Abraham knew it was a test or not remains unstated—God calls "Abraham!" the patriarch responds, "Here I am." The Hebrew, used here for the first time in the Bible, is *hineni*; the Greek is *idou egō*, literally, "Behold (or Look), I am." Abraham is present to God as he is to his son. Seven verses later, when "Isaac said to his father Abraham, 'Father!' Abraham responds, "Here I am, my son" (Genesis 22:7). The analogy is beautiful: we can be, should be, as present to God the Father as we as parents are to our children. The phrase occurs a third time in the chapter when Abraham is about to sacrifice his son. The "angel of the Lord" (likely the same one who called to Hagar in the wilderness in the previous chapter and assured her that she would not see the death of her son Ishmael) called to Abraham from heaven: "Abraham, Abraham!" Abraham responds, "Here I am" (Genesis 22:11). This is what it means to be obedient to God, whether the test or the salvation.

The response "Here I am" shows up another thirty or so times in the Bible. For our purposes, four more underscore the Gospel narrative. First, in Exodus 3:4, God calls to Moses from the burning bush, and Moses responds, "Here I am." This is the point where God commissions Moses to return to Egypt and tell Pharaoh to free the Hebrew slaves. Second, in 1 Samuel 3:4, set after Hannah has delivered her son to Eli at Shiloh, God calls to the child, "Samuel, Samuel," and the child responds, "Here I am." The ideal is that when God calls us by name, we respond, whether with trepidation or joy or perhaps a combination, "Here I am."

Third, God also responds, "Here I am." The relationship is reciprocal. Isaiah 58:9a explains, "Then you shall call, and the LORD will answer; / you shall cry for help, and he will say, 'Here I am.'" Alternatively, in Isaiah 65:1, the prophet speaks the words of God: "I was ready to be sought out by those who did not ask, / to be found by those who did not seek me. / I said, 'Here I am, here I am,' / to a nation that did not call on my name." This is the same chapter of Isaiah in which God speaks of creating "new heavens and a new earth" (Isaiah 65:17).

We can hear a faint echo of this response when Gabriel explains to Mary that she will give birth. She responds, "Behold" or "look" (*idou*), "the slave of the Lord" (Luke 1:38, my translation). The NRSVue strengthens the connection by translating "Here am I." The intertexts not only connect Mary to the ancient figures, they also connect the implications of her response. To be called by God does not usually signal a walk in the park. Abraham is initially called to sacrifice his son on the altar, as Mary will witness the death of her son on the cross. Moses, like Hagar, is called to return to slavery. Like Samuel and Jesus, he will face rejection, and he will attempt to lead a people who are not always inclined to listen to him. Mary connects herself to that ancient slavery, even as she will be aware that people will reject her son. As Simeon tells her when she presents baby Jesus in the Temple, "This child is destined for the falling and the rising of many in Israel and to be a sign that will be opposed..." (Luke 2:34).

The Circumcision of Jesus

Following the description of Ishmael's birth (Genesis 16:15-16), the text turns to the covenant that God establishes with Abraham and his posterity. The sign of that covenant is the circumcision of all male members of Abraham's household (Genesis 17:11-14). Immediately following that notification, God tells Abraham that regarding Sarah, "I will bless her and also give you a son by her. I will bless her, and she shall give rise to nations; kings of peoples shall come from her" (Genesis 17:16). Abraham expresses concern regarding Ishmael, and God tells him not to worry. God will also bless Ishmael and "make him a great nation" (Genesis 17:20). But the covenant will go through Sarah's son. After this revelation, Abraham arranges the circumcision of himself (at age ninety-nine), of Ishmael (aged thirteen), and of the other males in the household. The following scene, Genesis 18, is the visitors' annunciation that Abraham and Sarah will have a son.

In continuity with this covenant, Luke 1:59-64 reports how, on the eighth day after his birth, John was to be circumcised. Elizabeth insists that the child be named John (thus, Zechariah, who received the name from the angel, must have spoken with his wife). Shortly thereafter, Mary gives birth to

Jesus. Luke 2:21 reports, "When the eighth day came, it was time to circumcise the child, and he was called Jesus, the name given by the angel before he was conceived in the womb." There are not many sermons these days on the circumcision of any of these individuals.

Until 1960, a number of Christian churches celebrated the "Feast of the Circumcision of Christ" on January 1: The date is eight days after Christmas, and God instructed Abraham that all males born into his household should be circumcised on the eighth day after birth.

Granted, people have had other things to do aside from celebrating a circumcision on New Year's Day. On the other hand, the connection of this part of the Christmas story to Genesis should not be cut off (I couldn't resist). First, in medieval thought, the (very small amount of) blood shed during the circumcision process signaled the beginning of salvation, since as Paul puts it, "We have now been justified by his blood" (Romans 5:9). Second, the connection shows how the baby now embodies the covenant with Israel.

Third, and this a historical point that I find fascinating: to this day, Jewish boys are formally named at the time of their circumcision (our son Alexander was, to us, always Alexander, but to our synagogue he was formally "baby boy Geller" until his circumcision). Ironically, while this naming tradition is part of Jewish practice to this day, its *first* notice is actually the naming of John (the Baptist) in Luke 1:59, "On the eighth day they came to circumcise the child, and they were going to name him Zechariah after his father." The second notice is Luke 2:21,

"When the eighth day came, it was time to circumcise the child, and he was called Jesus, the name given by the angel before he was conceived in the womb."

Today, circumcision tends to be restricted to Jewish (and Muslim) religious practices, although there is some medical indication that it protects against a number of unpleasant medical concerns. Yet it helps us understand not only the Christmas story, but our own lives as well. For the New Testament Nativity accounts, it recollects the covenant with Abraham and the fidelity to that covenant of Elizabeth and Zechariah, Mary and Joseph. For people today, it can remind us of the stories our bodies tell, especially by tattooing or piercing or various forms of surgery. I remember, when I was a child, being fascinated by one of my father's friends from the Navy who had a ship tattooed on his arm. He could move his muscles in a way that made the ship look like it was pitching in the water. I also remember friends of my parents and of my grandmother who had numbers tattooed on their arms. No one talked about that. Bodies speak to our identities.

Finally, there are marks that are invisible, but we know they are there. Instead of concentrating on the painful ones, I'd prefer to think of the hidden but permanent mark of baptism. Some people remember their baptisms; others were baptized as infants; still others were baptized several times in different churches. Since in both Greek and Hebrew the expression we translate "running water" can also mean "living water," every time a drop of rain falls, or one turns on the faucet, could there be a reminder of baptism and a concern to recommit?

Retrospect

Book publishers and academics speak about "elevator pitches": summaries of books or dissertations that can be done in the quick movement between floors. If we were to do elevator pitches of what looking at the stories of the Old Testament contribute to the New, we'd be on that elevator for days. But quick run-throughs can get us started.

From the story of Hagar, we can better read the Nativity stories in relation to slavery and freedom and so to sin (a burden, a stain, a debt) and redemption (lifting off the burden, wiping away or covering over the stain, paying the debt). We can see how the stories relate both to Jews such as Joseph, Mary, and Jesus, but also to non-Jews such as the women in Matthew's genealogy, the magi, and the people in Egypt who provided shelter for Mary and Joseph. We can see the emphasis on *oni/ tapeinōsis*/humiliation/destitution and recognize the need for liberation from both spiritual/psychological as well as physical oppression. Hagar tells us that "God sees." Hagar, who also begins to see through her own eyes, both tells us that anyone can humiliate another, and anyone can be the agent of liberation.

Sarah not only reminds us of Elizabeth, she shows us that sometimes we turn our own oppression on others: what Abraham did to her regarding Pharaoh, she does to Hagar regarding Abraham. Her resentment of Hagar is palpable, and so she becomes for us the opportunity for identification and for intervention. The Bible invites us to see ourselves in all the characters, and in doing so learn from them. From Sarah we also learn about the joy of physical intimacy between older adults, as the cannons of the 1812 Overture shake the earth.

Samson's story also gives us comedy. There are serious moments in the Bible, but that is not all the Bible has to offer. If in reading the text we find ourselves smiling—at Sarah's comments regarding a forthcoming pregnancy, at Mrs. Manoah's conversation with the angel, and many more stories—we are more likely to see the laughter behind the Gospel's Christmas stories. Matthew's Joseph, son of Jacob, will remind us of that earlier Joseph, son of Jacob, who also dreamed dreams and took his family to Egypt to protect them, and recognition of that connection is joyful. We can find the humor in Luke's note that Mary put Jesus in a feeding trough (the famous "manger"), in anticipation that he will give his body as food. There is humor in the magi asking King Herod, the nominal "king of the Jews," about the location of the newborn "king of the Jews."

The story of Hannah gives us the importance of prayer. Jesus, too, will pray, and we can better understand how heart-felt his prayers are when we read him in light of Hannah. In Psalm 22 and other Lament Psalms, we can hear both Hannah and Jesus, and so we realize that we can pray these prayers ourselves. Eli gives us lessons in the problems of judging by appearances, the need for pastoral care, and the importance of assurance. He also tells us that sometimes children do not do what we would wish for them. Perhaps Samuel's righteousness filled in for him the loss he felt concerning his own unrighteous sons. Elkanah reminds me of Joseph. As Jesus tells Joseph that "his Father's house" is not the home Joseph made for the family in Nazareth, so Elkanah realizes, because of his wife's vow, that his son Samuel will not live with the family in their house in the hill country of Ephraim.

The story of Moses is the model for Jesus in Matthew 1–2 and indeed throughout the Gospel. The focus on the infancy material gives us stories of women, of courage, of cooperation, and of political subversion. Jesus knew, from stories of his ancestor David and from stories about Moses, that sometimes one has to fight for what one knows to be right. He knows that rejection is not the end of the story. He knows that God hears.

EPILOGUE

Continuing the Story

The stories of Moses, Miriam and Aaron, Amram and Jochebed, even of Pharaoh's daughter continue, both in the Bible and in postbiblical literature. Three of my favorites concern, respectively, Jochebed the biological mother who gave birth to, gave up, and then gave milk to Moses; Batya, Pharaoh's daughter, who raised the baby as her own in violation of her father's commands, and finally baby Moses himself.

According to the midrash known as *Deuteronomy Rabbah*, when the time came, at age 120, for Moses to die, he pleaded that his life be spared on behalf of his mother, who was still alive. Why, asks Moses, should his mother suffer not just the death of two of her children (Aaron and Miriam died during the Israelites' forty years in the wilderness) but also the death of her third? I have, thank heaven, never suffered the loss of a child, but I have friends who have. My mother miscarried several times before I was born, and I am an only child. When I was pregnant with Sarah, my mother sat me down and warned me about what could happen, not to frighten me (I already knew the possibilities of miscarriage) but to reassure me. One will always grieve the loss, whether of children who never took a breath or children who die before their parents, but one can live on in memory of that loss, just as one in the Jewish tradition says, to those who mourn, "May their memory be for a blessing." We can live in a way that honors the dead. Moses's prayer in the midrash was not granted, and he dies before his mother. According to another midrash (*Seder Olam Rabbah* 9), Jochebed enters the Promised Land. She carried the legacy of her children with her.

The second midrash concerns Pharaoh's daughter, who receives in later Jewish tradition the name Batya (sometimes spelled Bithiah) which means "daughter of God." (You may be familiar with the term *bat mitzvah*, literally, "daughter of the commandment.") *Leviticus Rabbah* 1:3 describes the origins of the name: God tells Pharaoh's daughter that because she raised Moses as her son although he was not her (biological) son, so she will be known as "my daughter" (God's daughter) although she is not God's biological daughter.

Less fancifully, the name may derive from one of those (seemingly endless) genealogies in the book of 1 Chronicles, which mentions, "The sons of Ezrah: Jether, Mered, Epher, and Jalon. These are the sons of Bithiah, daughter of Pharaoh, whom Mered married, and she conceived and bore Miriam, Shammai, and Ishbah father of Eshtemoa" (1 Chronicles 4:17).

Here are three of several reasons why this genealogy intrigues me. First, what is the daughter of Pharaoh doing married to a Jew (technically, a Judahite) man? The text looks like it is reporting an intermarriage, such as the marriage generations previously of Joseph to Aseneth, the daughter of the Egyptian priest Potiphera. Second, why does this Egyptian woman have a Hebrew name, or, for that matter, why do Moses and Miriam, and probably Aaron as well, along with Phinehas and Hophni, have Egyptian names? Do we understand them differently if we see their families as having assimilated? Third, who is this other Miriam in the genealogy? Was she named after Moses's sister, as Mary the mother of Jesus, Mary Magdalene, Mary the sister of Martha, and all the other first-century Jewish Marys may have been?

As for Batya, *Midrash Tadshe* includes a list of numerous Gentile women who entered paradise. Along with Batya are Hagar, Shiphrah and Puah, Aseneth the wife of Joseph, Zipporah the wife of Moses, Rahab the prostitute from Jericho who protected the Israelite spies, and Jael the wife of Heber the Kenite who aids Deborah the prophet during the period of the Judges. Like the Gentile magi who come to greet baby Jesus, the newborn "king of the Jews," so these Gentile women are mediators between the two communities. The Jewish tradition of the "righteous gentile" teaches that Jews do not have a lock on divine care, that godliness can be manifested by anyone regardless of ethnicity or gender, and people outside our community can also function as role models. One need not convert to Judaism in order to be righteous.

Jews, in general, did not think that Gentiles needed to become Jews in order to live a moral life or be in a right relationship with God. This perspective is shared by most ethnic groups: most Canadians, US citizens, and Mexicans do not think that only they are moral or beloved by God. Thus, Jews can honor, respect, and find to be moral exemplars those who are not Jews. Jesus would, I think, hold the same perspective, as we see with his interaction with Gentiles such as the Syro-Phoenician woman of Mark 7, the centurion in Matthew 8 and Luke 7, and the people at the feeding of the four thousand.

The third midrash, from *Exodus Rabbah* 1:26, concerns baby Moses. When Pharaoh's daughter receives Moses back from his biological mother and announces that she is going to raise him in the palace, the court magicians (we can think of them as political advisors whose job it is to read the signs of the times) suggest that the baby is a danger. It doesn't take a magician to arrive at this determination. Moses was a Hebrew, and the magicians likely feared that he would ally himself with his own people, now enslaved and oppressed. Pharaoh had already expressed his fears that the Hebrews "will increase and, in the event of war, join our enemies" (Exodus 1:10). The magicians, as court employees, do well to parrot the fears of their leader.

One of the magicians proposes a test: put in front of the baby a pot of hot coals and a pot of jewels and see which one he touches. If he goes for the jewels, then he is danger and should be dispatched. If he goes for the coals, he is not a danger. The test is set up, and the baby, as might be expected, reaches for the shining jewels. But Gabriel (yes, that Gabriel) pushes the child's hand toward the coals. Moses burns his finger, which he then puts to his lips, and that's how he comes to have a speech impediment (see Exodus 4:10).

A Child Is Born

According to the internet, a child is born every eight seconds. There's a website that gives the countdown of the number of births in the world per month. It's a lot. Thus, to say "a child is born" is same-old, same-old. Except to the child's parents, for whom this birth is something distinct, special, remarkable. The births of Isaac and Ishmael, Moses, Samson, Samuel, John, and Jesus, are all distinct, special, and remarkable. So are the births of Hagar and Sarah, Jochebed and Miriam, Mrs. Manoah, Hannah and Peninnah and their daughters—even if the Bible does not record their stories.

Advent is the time when we read about the baby Jesus. It can also be a time when we tell what stories we have of our own parents, what they or others told us about our births, our first memories, our first fears, or joys. These are stories that can be shared with friends, or passed down to children and grandchildren, or any in the next generations. Advent is thus not just a time to anticipate the future. It is like the Jewish new year, also a time to remember and to know that we are remembered.

Watch videos based on *A Child Is Born: A Beginner's Guide to Nativity Stories* with Amy-Jill Levine through Amplify Media.

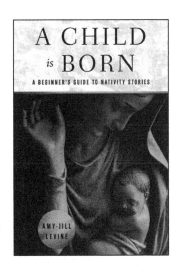

Amplify Media is a multimedia platform that delivers high quality, searchable content with an emphasis on Wesleyan perspectives for churchwide, group, or individual use on any device at any time. In a world of sometimes overwhelming choices, Amplify gives church leaders and congregants media capabilities that are contemporary, relevant, effective and, most importantly, affordable and sustainable.

With *Amplify Media* church leaders can:

- Provide a reliable source of Christian content through a Wesleyan lens for teaching, training, and inspiration in a customizable library
- Deliver their own preaching and worship content in a way the congregation knows and appreciates
- Build the church's capacity to innovate with engaging content and accessible technology
- Equip the congregation to better understand the Bible and its application
- Deepen discipleship beyond the church walls

Ask your group leader or pastor about Amplify Media and sign up today at www.AmplifyMedia.com.